DATE DUE

FOREWORD

"Frontiers of America" dramatizes some of the explorations and discoveries of real pioneers in simple, uncluttered text. America's spirit of adventure is seen in these early people who faced dangers and hardship blazing trails, pioneering new water routes, becoming Western heroes as well as legends, and building log forts and houses as they settled in the wilderness.

Although today's explorers and adventurers face different frontiers, the drive and spirit of these early pioneers in America's past still serve as an inspiration.

ABOUT THE AUTHOR

During her years as a teacher and reading consultant in elementary schools, Mrs. McCall developed a strong interest in the people whose pioneering spirit built our nation. When she turned to writing as a full-time occupation, this interest was the basis for much of her work. She is the author of many books and articles for children and adults, and co-author of elementary school social studies textbooks.

Frontiers of America

FORTS IN THE WILDERNESS

By Edith McCall

Illustrations by Darrell Wiskur

CP CHILDRENS PRESS, CHICAGO

exploration

—————— La SALLE

··········· CLARK

Library of Congress Cataloging in
Publication Data
McCall, Edith S.
    Forts in the wilderness
    1.   Northwest, Old—History—Juvenile
literature.   2.   Fortification—Northwest, Old—
Juvenile literature.   [1.   Northwest, Old—
History.   2.   Fortification—Northwest, Old]
I.   Wiskur, Darrell.   II.   Title.
F479.3.M3   977   68-15807
ISBN 0-516-03324-7

Cover photograph courtesy
of James P. Rowan

New 1980 Edition
Copyright© 1968 by Regensteiner
Publishing Enterprises, Inc.
All rights reserved. Published
simultaneously in Canada.
Printed in the United States of America.
1 2 3 4 5 6 7 8 9 10 11 12 R 87 86 85 84 83 82 81 80

CONTENTS

LASALLE MEETS
THE ILLINOIS INDIANS

A worried frown was on the face of the dark-haired young man as he tried to see through the curtain of powdery snow that had begun to fall on that December day of the year 1679. He left the group of about thirty men who were huddled around the eight canoes that had been drawn up onto the bank of the St. Joseph River, about where South Bend, Indiana, is today.

As he walked along the bank of the river, running black now under the wintry sky, the young man struck a gloved hand against a bare one. The glove hid an iron hook, for he had lost one hand a few years earlier, when he had been a soldier in the Italian army and a grenade had exploded as he held it. The young man's name was Henry de Tonty, but people spoke of him as "Tonty of the Iron Hand."

"Tonty!" he heard, and looked back. A big-framed man was hurrying after him, pulling a gray robe close about his body to keep out the cold. He was Father Hennepin, one of the three priests who had come into this wilderness to teach the Indians about Christianity. Father Hennepin had to let go of his robe to keep from falling as he slipped on the muddy riverbank in his hurry to catch up with Tonty. "Tonty, don't you disappear, too," he said. "It is enough that LaSalle has been gone for many hours now."

Tonty turned back. "I am worried, Father Hennepin," he said. "LaSalle should have been back long ago. Something must have happened to him in the woods. I want to look for him, but the snow has covered his tracks."

Father Hennepin tried to peer into the dim wilderness up the river as daylight faded. He shuddered. "Don't go, Tonty. You must not leave the men, or they will turn about and go back. All that LaSalle has done so far will be wasted. Surely he will find his way back any minute now, with news that he has found the path to the headwaters of the rivers of the Illinois Country."

Tonty turned and walked back toward the cluster of canoes and the men who sat nearby, wrapped in their blankets. The slender boats were heavily loaded. Along with blankets, cloth and an assortment of other goods for trading with Indians, they held an iron forge and blacksmith's tools, saws, hammers and other carpenter's tools, guns, lead and gunpowder. All had been brought almost the full length of Lake Michigan, from a French outpost at Green Bay. Big, handsome Robert Cavalier de LaSalle, the man Tonty waited for now, had brought the canoes this far. He and the fourteen men with him had weathered terrible storms on Lake Michigan. They had lived through days when the men could find nothing to eat but the remains of a deer already picked over by buzzards, and some wild berries that made them ill. They had met unfriendly Indians, and it had taken all of LaSalle's skill as a leader to convince the Indians that the explorers meant no harm and should be allowed to go free.

Now, after being joined at the St. Joseph River by Tonty and seventeen more men, LaSalle was trying to find the way to the country of the Illinois Indians, hoping to get there before winter blocked the way. There, LaSalle planned, he would build a chain of forts and start a fur-trading business greater than all that the French had built in Canada. And he, Robert Cavalier de LaSalle, would go all the way to the mouth of the great Mississippi River, as no Frenchman had yet done. There he would begin to build a city, a great port that would make the heartland of

North America a monument to the glory of France.

In the morning of this day in early December, LaSalle had taken his trusted friend, Tonty, to one side when the men had reached a sharp bend in the St. Joseph River.

"I am sure, Tonty," LaSalle said, "that this is as far as we should follow the St. Joseph. We must go westward to the headwaters of the rivers of the Illinois Country. But I am not certain of the trail. I will go find the portage and be back in an hour or so."

A portage is the part of a river journey in which the men must carry the canoes and all the goods overland from one river to another. LaSalle had brought with him a Mohican Indian who had traveled this way before and knew the portage route, but the Mohican had gone off, hunting wild game for food.

Hours had passed and LaSalle had not returned. "Make camp for the night," Tonty ordered as he reached the men. He appointed some to stand guard while the others slept. "Fire three rounds each hour," he said. "If Sieur de LaSalle can hear the shots, he will be guided back to us."

A gray dawn broke at last. "Now he will come," Tonty thought. But the hours dragged by, with no sign of LaSalle. Tonty knew that soon he must lead the men onward himself. The Mohican hunter had returned, and could show the way to the portage. Noon came, and still Tonty did not order the men to start.

Tonty told Father Hennepin, "I will wait out the day. If LaSalle does not return, we will be on our way with the first streak of daylight."

It was about four o'clock when one of the men saw a dark figure approaching the camp, coming along the riverbank.

"It's Sieur de LaSalle!" he shouted. But the man who approached looked very little like the French nobleman they all knew, the man who dressed as if for an appearance before the king even in the heart of the wilderness. LaSalle's face and hands were black with charcoal smears. He had two opossums hanging from his belt. He had killed them with a stick as they hung by their tails from a tree limb, to save in case he needed more food.

"LaSalle, my good friend!" cried Tonty. "I feared you were dead!"

"Dead? Not I," said LaSalle. "I have too much yet to do in this world to be ready to move on to the next so soon."

He told Tonty how he had lost his way the day before, after being forced to circle a swampy area. In the snow, he could not even find his way back to the river until he chanced upon it in the night. He had fired his gun, but heard no answer from Tonty. So he had moved along the riverbank until he saw the gleam of a campfire.

"I was sure I had found our camp, and hurried into it. To my surprise, no one was there. It had not been deserted for long, for a heap of dry grass was still warm from some unknown sleeper whom I must have disturbed with my gunfire. An Indian, no doubt," he said.

LaSalle, after his arrival in Canada in 1666, when he was just twenty-three years old, had learned much of the ways of the Indians, and had learned to speak several Indian tongues. "Not wanting to lose my scalp," he went on, "I called out in several Indian languages, but there was not a sound. So I shouted that I was about to make myself comfortable on that warm couch, built up a wall of brush about me so that no one could creep up on me in silence, rebuilt the fire, and went to sleep. Now let's get on with the portage."

The men shouldered the heavy loads and followed the Mohican. They camped when darkness forced them to do so. LaSalle was so weary that he narrowly

escaped being burned in his sleep in the little wigwam that he and Father Hennepin had built of reed mats and were sharing. The cold was so great that they built a small fire inside the tent. But the wind whipped it into a blaze before daybreak, setting the mats afire.

This began their day. They tramped across five miles of dreary, flat land, half covered with snow and dotted with the whitened bones and skulls of buffalo. They could see a Miami Indian camp in the distance. The Indians did not try to stop them, but one of LaSalle's own men, who held a grudge against his leader, almost brought an end to LaSalle's life.

He was walking behind LaSalle when another man saw him getting his rifle ready for firing. As the man aimed the gun at LaSalle's back, the second man yelled, "Sire! Step aside!" At the same time, he seized the gun barrel and forced it upward.

LaSalle's eyes burned in anger at the traitor, and he wanted to order him shot. But he needed every man, and ordered the march to go on. At last they came to the thread of water that was the beginning of the Kankakee River, the stream that would take them to the Illinois River, an important branch of the Mississippi. At first the stream was so narrow that a man could leap over it, but at last the canoes were afloat once more. The river wound through marshy land. The men were grateful that the weather was cold enough to give them frozen ground upon which to camp for the night.

A few days later, the land became a rolling plain where hoofprints of buffalo could be seen. But the Mohican could find no buffalo to kill for food. The herds had moved south as the wintry weather came. He found only two lean deer and a few wild geese. The hungry, weary men began to grumble. For most of them, this was the first long trip into the wilderness. They were carpenters and blacksmiths, not woodsmen.

"I came to build forts and ships, not to starve or freeze at the end of the world," one of them said. Others echoed his words. The man who tried to shoot LaSalle was seen talking with some of the most discontented.

"Some morning we may find that some of them have left us in the night," LaSalle said to Tonty. Tonty began having men he could trust stand guard at night.

There had been very little to eat for a week when the Mohican hunter came hurrying back to camp one day. "I need six men!" he called out. "I have found meat. A great buffalo bull caught in a swamp could not free himself to follow the herd."

Spirits lifted as the men smelled the great roasts that soon were turning on sticks over campfires. The sizzling of the fat was music to their ears.

The countryside improved as they journeyed on. They reached the place where the Des Plaines River from the north joined the Kankakee to form the Illinois River. The men paddled along between grassy meadows, broken by rises of land with groves of trees. There were wooded islands in the river, with plenty of fuel for campfires. The men were in better spirits — all but LaSalle himself.

"The real test is still to come," he told his trusted friend Tonty. "The reports of Louis Jolliet and Father Marquette, who came this way six years ago, tell of a great Indian settlement just down the river from here. All the people of the Illinois tribes have lodges there, and plant corn in fields near the town. From there, they go out on long hunting journeys."

"Why does this worry you?" asked Tonty. "You have dealt often with the Indians in Canada."

LaSalle said, "Ah — but that is where the trouble lies. You know that I have made treaties with the Iroquois tribes south of the St. Lawrence Valley. The

Iroquois are known as the fiercest fighters of all, and they have been sending war parties to the Ohio and Illinois countries. The Illinois are Algonkian people, enemies of the Iroquois. They fear a great war with the Iroquois. These Indians just ahead of us may have heard of my work to form a friendship with the Iroquois. They may look upon us as enemies sent by the Iroquois. If so, we will have trouble."

"I understand," said Henry de Tonty. "But you are wise in the ways of the Indian. I have faith that you will know how to meet the Illinois chiefs, my good friend."

"Thank you, Tonty," said LaSalle. "Mind you, now — let no hint of my fears reach our men. Nor shall I act as if I expected any trouble when I meet the Illinois chiefs. They remember Father Marquette, I am sure, and looked upon him as a true friend. Perhaps, bcause we are also French, they will welcome us."

Tonty smiled. "I believe that is how it will be. Our only worry is to keep our men's stomachs filled. With full stomachs, the men will follow where you lead them and obey your orders."

LaSalle's frown deepened again. "That is not so easy, Tonty. We are in need of a winter's supply of food. I hope to buy corn from the Illinois tribes. We should reach the towns in a day or two, and I hope there has been a good harvest and that Indians will be there to sell us some corn. But the tribes may not yet have returned from the fall hunting trips."

The next day, as the canoes came from behind an island, the men sighted a great rock cliff on the left bank. It rose straight up from the water, about one hundred twenty-five feet. Its top was quite flat, about seventy feet broad, and crowned with trees.

LaSalle said, "Father Marquette told of this great rock. It was here that he came in the spring of 1675, four and a half years ago. See, off to the right across the river from the Great Rock — there lie the Illinois towns! The good Father preached an Easter sermon there, only a few weeks before he died."

LaSalle gazed intently at the town, but he saw no movement among the lodges. No smoke rose from the holes in the roofs. No people came from the buildings as the canoes drew near the settlement.

Soon all the canoes were tied to low-hanging limbs along the right bank. LaSalle called a greeting in an Algonkian tongue. He waited for a reply, but none came.

"They have not returned from the fall hunt," he said to Tonty. "We will have to do something about food. We can't go on without a supply to carry us through the rest of the winter."

He told the men they could go ashore, but not to do anything that might be looked upon by the Indians as an unfriendly act. Soon all were walking along the deserted streets and peering into some of the hundreds of lodges. Each was large enough to house two or three families. They were shaped like loaves of bread, made of thick grasses and rushes woven over a framework of poles. Beyond the deserted lodges there were great fields in which dry cornstalks stood, and where a few pumpkins and squashes clung to frost-withered vines.

"Look here, Sire!" one of the men called to LaSalle. "Here is a pit, full of corn." He had lifted a thin layer of sod from the ground and pulled back a deerhide beneath the soil. "Why can't we just take the corn and leave?"

"We shall take the corn," LaSalle said, "but not without putting payment for it in the pit in its place. To steal it would bring certain death to us as soon as the owners discovered what we had done."

More pits were found. LaSalle directed the men as they loaded a supply of corn into the canoes, and put trading goods into the pits in exchange. Soon the

canoes were moving down the river, and the Great
Rock and the Indian city disappeared from view.

Four days later, on January 5, 1680, they rounded
a great bend in the Illinois River, where the river's
flow changed from mostly westward to a generally
southward direction. Soon the river had widened into
a lake, narrowing again at the place where Peoria,
Illinois, now is. The explorers passed this place about
nine in the morning of a crisp, wintry day.

"Sire!" called Tonty to LaSalle from the canoe in
which he rode. He waved with his gloved hand, and
LaSalle saw that columns of smoke were rising from

the woods just beyond a bend in the river, seeming to come from camps on both shores.

Only someone close to LaSalle would have noticed the tightening of the muscles about his mouth and known that he felt any fear. Calmly, he said to the men in his canoe, "We are about to meet the returning Illinois Indian hunters. Pass the word along to the other canoes that we must be ready for action. Follow my lead in what you do."

He ordered all the canoes pulled abreast of each other, forming a line across the river. LaSalle stood in the bow of the canoe nearest the left bank, from which more smoke was rising and where it was likely the larger camp was located. Tonty was in the bow of the canoe nearest the right bank.

"Have your rifles ready, but don't fire unless I order it," LaSalle told the men. "And no matter how much fear you feel, don't let it show on your face or in your actions. Indians respect men of courage."

In silence, the men obeyed. The canoes rounded a last small bend in the river and were in open view of Indian camps on both shores. Instantly, there were shouts and screams from the Indians. Women and children and even some of the men ran from the campfires toward the woods, in terror at the sight of the rifles pointed towards them.

"Now!" cried LaSalle. He leaped ashore. Tonty, at the right bank, did the same. Most of the men followed LaSalle or Tonty, leaving just one man in each canoe to tend the boat. Each man, as he landed, pointed his rifle toward the Indians and stood in silence, as LaSalle was doing.

The screaming had stopped. Indians and explorers stood facing each other in a moment that seemed frozen in time. LaSalle's eyes met those of the chief. Not a flicker betrayed the Frenchman's thoughts. Did the chief know that if the rifles were fired that the explorers could be seized in the time it would take to reload? Did he realize how few explorers there were against his hundreds of Indian braves?

The moment ended. The chief motioned with his hand to the lesser chiefs who stood near him. Then he took the feather-decorated clay pipe, the calumet of peace, that was handed to him and held it toward LaSalle. He said something to one of his followers, who signaled to the Indians across the river who stood ready to attack with bows and arrows. LaSalle lowered his rifle, and Tonty, on the other shore, did the same. But neither man allowed the relief he felt to show upon his face.

LaSalle had another calumet in readiness inside his shirt. He pulled it out and held it toward the chief. Father Hennepin, breathing a great sigh of relief, walked toward a group of children peering fearfully from behind their mother. He laid a gentle hand on a child's head, smiling as he did so.

"We come in peace to meet our brothers," LaSalle said. His voice was firm as he spoke in an Algonkian tongue the chief appeared to understand. The moment he had dreaded had passed, but much depended upon how he handled the conversations that were to come. Did these Indians believe he had come from the dreaded enemy, the Iroquois? Was the chief's welcome just a pretense, to give the Indians time to catch the explorers off guard?

FIRST FORT
IN THE WILDERNESS

Before long, the Indian chiefs had a feast of welcome underway. The Frenchmen were seated in a circle, food placed before them, and their feet warmed and rubbed with bear grease. When one of the men drew back as a squaw knelt before him to rub his feet, LaSalle frowned at him.

"Allow them to do as they will, Joseph. It is a sign of welcome, and they will not understand if any man refuses," he said in French. Then he called to one of the men who stood near the canoes.

"Beach the canoes. Then bring that chest to me," he ordered.

From the chest, LaSalle took bundles of tobacco and some hatchets, shipped from France. With great ceremony, he presented them to the chief.

"I have come," he told the men who sat in council later in the day, "to protect you against your enemies. I shall build strong walls. From behind them, we shall together fight off any who might come to disturb your cities or to hunt in your grounds. The Great Father in France, our King, wants to take care of you."

He told the chiefs also of the stop he and his men had made at the deserted city, and gave more bolts of cloth in payment for the corn the men had taken. The chiefs seemed satisfied.

"There will be more gifts for you, many many more," LaSalle said. "I will build a great canoe. In it, we will sail to the waters where the sun rises and bring back the riches of France."

When he saw looks of doubt upon the faces of the chiefs, LaSalle hinted that the Osage Indians farther to the west would be most happy to have all the gifts, perhaps including some of the white men's guns. This settled the matter. The Illinois chiefs assured LaSalle that a strong friendship was between them and the Frenchmen. The feasting went on, with dancing and great ceremony, far into the night. Then the Frenchmen were invited to sleep in one of the best wigwams.

It took a long time for sleep to come to Robert LaSalle, even though he had slept on the ground on an Indian mat of rushes many times before. But at last he dropped off into a restless sleep. It seemed to him in the night that he heard voices, low and guarded, and heard men moving about.

"It must have been a dream," he decided in the morning. But soon he knew something had happened in the night. Indians watched the Frenchmen constantly.

"Why do you not trust me this day as you did last night?" LaSalle asked the chief. "Have you already forgotten that we smoked the calumet as brothers?"

The chief seemed uncomfortable, but he did not explain.

A short time later, one of the braves, pretending to guard LaSalle, walked with him to the canoes. He pointed out a fine steel knife, and said, "For that knife, I will tell you of the reason for the clouds over your head this morning."

"Speak," said LaSalle.

The Indian told him that in the night six Miami Indians had come to the camp. The chiefs had been called into council. The leader of the Miami, whose name was Monso, had warned the Illinois against LaSalle.

"He is a friend of the Iroquois," Monso had said. "Do not believe his words. He is on his way to the other side of the Great River. There he will get the tribes to band together to return and make war on you. At the same time, the Iroquois will come from the East. You shall be crushed between them as I crush this glowworm between two stones. Your light shall go out forever."

The Indian told LaSalle that Monso had refused to lie down with his Illinois brothers, but had left while darkness still blanketed the camp.

In the afternoon, the Frenchmen were invited to a feast in the chief's lodge. Each sat on a mat, with his hunting knife in his hand and a wooden bowl before him, ready to receive a chunk of meat and some corn that had been boiled in fat. But before the food was brought in, the chief arose.

"My white brothers must go no farther," he said, after a long opening speech full of polite words that meant little. "There is much danger ahead. The great river-to-the-sea is a trap of which I must warn you. It is ready to swallow all Frenchmen who enter its waters."

He described whirlpools that would break the greatest of canoes into sticks, rocks that would crush the bones of any man who should be hurled against them. He spoke of waterfalls that would pull the ships into themselves, and where serpents were hiding to feast upon the living bodies of the men.

As the chief talked, LaSalle watched his men's faces.

"They believe him, and fear is written upon their faces," he thought. "They do not understand all the words, but they know he describes great dangers ahead."

Seeming to be very calm, LaSalle arose to reply to the chief. "I thank you for your deep concern, my brother," he said. "But we are not men to back off from danger, no matter how great. And now I must tell you that I did not sleep through the secret council of last night. I know of the visit of the man Monso, and of the story he told you."

LaSalle stopped speaking. He looked the chief in the eye, staring at him in silence until at last the chief lowered his gaze. Then LaSalle said, "If Monso told the truth, why did he not stay to face me? Why did he leave in the dark, like a cowardly animal afraid to face the light of day?"

No one spoke for a full minute. LaSalle drew the keen edge of his hunting knife across his thumb, as if testing its sharpness. Still holding it, he said, "Brother, I will tell you why! Monso was not telling the truth. He was twisting you about like a serpent

29

who has you in his coils, and his words came through a forked tongue!"

LaSalle paused. The chief looked up, an angry light in his eye. LaSalle looked again at his knife and then put it into its sheath. He said quietly, "You know, my brother, that we could have killed you all as we came into your camp, had we wanted to do so. We do not need the help of the Iroquois, or of any tribes to the west. The white man has magic that makes him more powerful than all his Indian brothers put together. But we did not come to use that power against you. We brought you gifts, and we wish to bring you many more, and to live in peace beside you.

"I will face this Monso and force the truth from him. Send for him, if you think I do not speak the truth. Bring him back. See if he can stand before me and tell his lies."

LaSalle sat down. Not a word was spoken. At last the chief grunted, and then signaled for the food to be brought in.

LaSalle was not sure of what might happen next. Most of his men slept in one lodge, and that night he ordered six of them to stand guard to see that the others were not attacked as they slept. But in the morning, all six guards had disappeared.

"Two of my best carpenters were among them," LaSalle groaned to Tonty. "They believed those stories the chief told them."

Tonty shook his head. "We can't spare a single man, if we are going to build forts and a ship. Those fools — how do they think they are going to live in the wilderness in the winter? And if the weather doesn't bring them down, do they think that the Indians will let them go free?"

LaSalle called his men together. "Those six cowards will die before they can go ten miles, if not of the Indian's arrow, then surely of cold and starvation. If any of the rest of you have such plans, wait until spring. Then you can return to Canada if you choose, and be given the means you need to get there.

"We shall not try to go to the Mississippi until all the ice is gone. Indeed we cannot, for we must first build our ship, not far from here. When it is finished, no man shall be forced to go on with me who does not freely choose to do so."

Convinced that they were safer staying together, the rest of the men went on with LaSalle and Tonty to a spot of higher ground a little farther down the river. At the same time, the Indians broke camp and continued upstream to their city across from the Great Rock.

Soon trees were being cut and shaped to form a palisade of pointed logs for the first fort of the Illinois Country. But LaSalle's heart was heavy, even as he watched its sturdy form take shape, overlooking the river on one side and rising above steep ravines behind it. LaSalle needed the men who had deserted. He also was worried about money. He had borrowed a great deal to pay for this expedition.

The summer before coming to the Illinois Country, LaSalle had built a ship on the Niagara River and launched it on Lake Erie. The *Griffin,* first ship to sail the Great Lakes, had carried LaSalle into Lake Huron and then to Lake Michigan, as far as Green Bay. He had sent it back to Niagara with a load of furs. The furs were to bring the needed money. The *Griffin* had had plenty of time to complete the trip, and a messenger should have reached LaSalle before he left the St. Joseph River. No messenger had come. The messenger also was to have brought rigging for the new ship.

LaSalle was heavy hearted even as he watched the walls rise for the first white man's building in Illinois. He named it *Fort Crevecoeur,* French for "broken-heart."

TONTY FACES THE IROQUOIS

By the last day of February, 1680, the oaken ribs of a new ship stood white against the forest darkness in a clearing on the bank of the Illinois River. On that day, Father Hennepin and two other men left in a canoe to go down the Illinois to the Mississippi River.

"You will be of great aid to me in bringing back reports of your journey," LaSalle said to Father Hennepin. "We will then know what to expect when we launch our ship." The next day, LaSalle himself set out in the opposite direction. With the Mohican hunter and four other men, he was taking two canoes back to Canada to get the rigging and other things needed in order to finish the ship.

"My good friend," LaSalle said as he took Tonty's hand. "It won't be easy to wait here, I know. I shall be thinking of you constantly until the day I see you again."

Tonty smiled a farewell, but he was uneasy. He knew that most of the fifteen workmen left to him were waiting for the day when they, too, could go back to Canada. Only two of them could be counted on as truly loyal — Jean, a boy in his late teens, and a young French nobleman named Etienne Renault. Of course, there were also the two priests, but neither was very strong.

About three weeks after LaSalle had left, as the new leaves were beginning to bud out on some of the bushes and the willow stems were turning red with the rising sap of springtime, a canoe arrived from upriver. Tonty recognized the two men in it as those who had remained at the mouth of the St. Joseph River to await a late message from the *Griffin*. "Hallo!" they called out, and the men crowded around them eagerly as they came ashore.

"Did LaSalle send our pay?" the newcomers were asked.

They shook their heads. "Things look bad," said one of them, whose name was LaChapelle. "The *Griffin* is lost. LaSalle is having a hard time trying to make up for the loss of that ship and all the furs that were on it."

The other man, Leblanc, had handed Tonty a letter from LaSalle.

"Should you decide it would be better, my trusted

friend," LaSalle had written, "go to the great rock that we observed as we came down the river, and build a fortress atop the rock. It is an excellent place, right across the river from the great Illinois towns and with a view of all that goes on for miles."

"I believe I shall go up to the Great Rock to look it over," Tonty told the men. He set out the next day with a few men. But he had not yet reached the Great Rock when Etienne Renault and Jean came paddling after him.

"They took everything they could carry," Etienne told Tonty. "The furs, the lead, the gunpowder — and then they set fire to the fort. Fort Crevecoeur is gone."

Tonty's heart sank. He had now only five workmen, the two priests, and the two who had come with the bad news. He ordered the canoes beached while he planned what to do.

"LaSalle must be told," he decided. He wrote two letters, chose two men to carry one of them to Canada by one route, and another pair to take the second one by a different route. He and those that were left of his little band went up to the Illinois villages, where about eight thousand Indians were living at the time. The chiefs gave them lodges to live in, near the city's edge, while they waited for word to come from LaSalle.

Tonty made one trip back to the ruined fort. The ship still stood. On one of the boards words had been scrawled in charcoal by one of the deserters: *Nous sommes tous sauvages.*

"Yes," thought Tonty, "we are all savages. At heart, each man seems to care most about himself and not about how he hurts his fellowman." His heart as heavy as the iron forge he loaded into his canoe, along with a few tools that remained, Tonty went back to the Indian town.

The summer passed and September came. Still there was no word from LaSalle. In the hot sunshine, Tonty paced impatiently before the hut where he and his last three men lived. The two priests were living outside the village. They had spent all the summer trying to make Christians of the Illinois Indians, and were quite discouraged because they had not succeeded.

On the morning of September 10, Tonty saw the squaws go to work in the fields, as usual. It was a hazy, lazy day, and many of the young men stretched out to sleep in the warm sunshine. It was too early to begin the fall hunt. A large company of braves had gone to war, leaving the younger, inexperienced men and the older warriors to guard the city. A few of the young braves and some of the older men sat around buffalo skins spread out on the ground, smooth side up, rolling cherry stones on it in a game of chance.

Restlessly, Tonty walked about the village. Then he turned and walked to the outlying land, where the graveyard was located. There, some of the dead were buried, and others, wrapped in skins, were laid on top of pole frameworks, high enough to keep the wolves from getting them. The sight always made Tonty shudder a little, and he turned back to join the other Frenchmen at their hut. He found them looking almost like Indians themselves, squatting in the sunshine, slapping at fleas. Etienne looked up as Tonty approached.

"If we don't get word in the next week, we shall start up the river to try to find LaSalle," Tonty announced. The others grunted approval of this idea, but had little to say. Tonty stirred up the cooking fire and started some water boiling to cook corn for the noon meal. There once had been cries of "Squaw work!" when Tonty and the young boy, Jean, were seen doing the cooking. Tonty had whirled about instantly and struck one blow at the nearest taunter, with his iron hand. The Indian fell, stunned. After that, the braves did not chance being hit with the gloved hand that was "medicine," to them — a word that meant the same as magic.

"Get some more wood," Tonty told Jean. As the lad was gathering an armload of sticks, the camp came suddenly alive and he ran back empty-handed. Women shrieked as they came running from the fields. Their children flocked around them. Every young man was on his feet, spreading the word to get ready for war. Tonty hurried towards the heart of the village to learn what was happening. He found that a young Shawnee Indian, who had left two days before to go back to his home country to the east, had returned. He brought startling news. A great band of Iroquois, in full war dress, were on their way.

Tonty stopped a few feet from the crowd gathering in the heart of the Indian city, just as his fellow Frenchmen came hurrying up to see what was happening.

"They brought the Iroquois upon us!" one brave was shouting, pointing towards the Frenchmen.

Suddenly the mob was turning towards the little group, shouting and angry.

"No," cried Tonty. "LaSalle would not send the

Iroquois to attack his own men! And you know I have not been away from this city for a long, long time." The crowd pushed in upon him, and Tonty raised his gloved hand, his "medicine." Not wanting to be struck, those who were nearest pushed back.

"Follow me!" shouted one young brave, and away he ran toward the lodge where Tonty and his men lived. The Frenchmen could only watch helplessly as the precious iron forge, the tools, and almost everything else they owned were carried from the lodge and flung into the Illinois River.

This seemed to satisfy the angry Indians and they had more important business to attend to. Soon they were pushing their big wooden dugout canoes into the river. Each one carried a full load of women and children, the mats they would need to put up tents, and a supply of food. About sixty men went with the women and children as protectors. They paddled the canoes downstream about ten miles to a place where there was a meadow on the right bank. This meadow was almost surrounded by marshes on the sides away from the river, making it an island.

When night came, only the warriors and the Frenchmen were left in the city across from the Great Rock. The braves built fires along the riverbank, forming an almost solid wall of flame. There was no quiet in the hours of darkness, for the warriors, now painted and with feathers in their hair, beat their drums, shouted, danced and leaped about through the hours of night.

As dawn came, a group of young warriors who had been sent upriver as scouts returned.

"Frenchmen bring Iroquois upon us!" they cried, excitedly. Again the accusing fingers pointed to Tonty. The scouts had seen two men they believed to be Frenchmen among the Iroquois. One wore a broad-brimmd hat such as the priests wore. The other was dressed in the type of European clothing that LaSalle always wore. The scouts were sure that LaSalle himself had returned, leading the warring Iroquois.

"Our end has come," Etienne Renault whispered to Tonty.

"Don't let them see you are frightened," warned Tonty. "That is one of the most important things I learned from LaSalle. Act like a coward and they'll kill you."

He walked calmly toward the shouting Indians and held up his gloved hand. "I will use this to fight at the side of my Illinois brothers!" he cried, and ran with the surprised braves to the water's edge where the canoes were drawn up. Soon they were on their way to met the Iroquois.

The scouts had reported that the enemy was coming down the Vermilion River, which flowed from the southeast and joined the Illinois downstream below the Great Rock. Soon the canoes were beached, and the men were running across the rolling plain above the Vermilion. About one hundred Illinois braves had guns. The rest were armed only with bows and arrows, and of course, their knives.

They had not far to go before they could see the enemy band, cutting across the plain, coming toward them as they left the woods along the Vermilion. The Iroquois were leaping, shouting, and firing guns as they advanced.

Tonty, in the front ranks of the Illinois warriors, thought, "This little band is no match for those fighters." He decided to try to stop the battle before it began. Perhaps the fact that the French and the Iroquois had signed a treaty to keep peace between them might be used now to help. He ran ahead of the Illinois, then turned and faced them, shouting and raising his gloved hand to get attention.

"I'm going to talk to them!" he said. "Here, Etienne, take my gun." He placed it on the ground.

"No, Tonty — no!" cried Etienne. "They'll shoot you before you've gone ten feet!"

But Tonty, waving a white wampum belt to show that he came in peace, was on his way toward the Iroquois. Bullets whizzed by him, but he was not hit, and as he drew near, an Iroquois chief ordered a halt.

In a moment, Tonty was the center of a group of writhing, painted warriors. He could feel their hot breath upon him, and all about him were small black eyes, shining with the fever of excitement. The Iroquois thought he was an Indian, for he had dark hair, grown long now, and he dressed as the Indians did. They were amazed that an Illinois brave would have the courage to run unarmed into their lines, but they soon recovered enough from their surprise to fight among themselves for the honor of killing him.

Tonty could not remember later how he lived through that moment when his life hung in the balance. A heavy blow fell on his head from behind him. He staggered, but forced himself to remain standing, although the painted faces about him became a blur of black and red. He felt the knife tip of one of the warriors cut through his clothing, and knew the searing pain as it pierced the flesh between his ribs. He steadied himself to make a last effort, and cried out in French to the chief.

The chief shouted one word, and the braves stopped, knives and tomahawks raised. They were so close about him that Tonty could not fall, though his knees were buckling. The chief pushed back one of the braves and put his face close to Tonty's. Then he turned Tonty's head and looked at one of his ears.

"His ears are not pierced," he cried in an Iroquois tongue. "He must be a Frenchman. Hold back!"

Tonty, fighting the humming and spinning in his head, felt himself lifted and carried a few feet to an open area. As the Iroquois braves put him down, Tonty was coughing blood. The Indians did their best to stop the hot, sticky flow from between his ribs, and in a few minutes he could gasp out a few words.

"Do not fight the Illinois. They are under the protection of your father, the king of France, and your brother, the governor of Canada. They will punish you."

A young brave came whooping by and snatched Tonty's hat from where it had fallen when he met the chief. He put it on the bayonet that tipped his gun, and holding it high, ran shouting back through the line to the thick of the battle that had broken out while Tonty was being carried away.

Etienne Renault, seeing his leader's hat, was sure that Tonty was dead. So were the Illinois braves who saw it, and they cried out, "Iron Hand is dead!"

It was almost the truth. While the Iroquois chiefs argued about what to do, one of the braves seized Tonty by the hair. He had his knife ready to scalp the Frenchman when one of the chiefs wheeled about and shoved him back.

Another chief had come into the group. He was an Onondaga, and had been present when LaSalle had signed a treaty with his people. "Let Iron Hand go free!" he argued. A chief of another of the Iroquois tribes, a Seneca, cried, "Keep him alive so that we can burn him!"

Tonty, half conscious, heard the jumble of voices over him. With all the strength he could gather, he tried to stand up. Indian hands grasped his arms. When he could speak, he said, "Don't give your lives here. These are only the Illinois scouts. Twelve hundred warriors are coming to surround you. Sixty Frenchmen wait to see if I return, ready to join in the battle. You must let me go back."

This brought a moment of silence and then a loud outburst of arguing among the chiefs. The Onondaga chief won out. He handed Tonty a white wampum belt. The Indians turned Tonty toward the battle line. Staggering, holding the belt as high as he could, Tonty went toward the Illinois lines. Chiefs shouted orders. The battlefield grew almost quiet. Tonty, scarcely able to stand, went slowly across the grassy plain, trampled now and littered with fallen braves.

The two French priests, who had crossed the river after the Illinois warriors, pushed their way through the mass of painted men. They ran to Tonty. Each took an arm. As the world again went black, Tonty felt himself being almost carried back toward the river.

The Illinois, glad of an excuse to turn away from a battle they were sure to lose, shouted last threats at the Iroquois and ran for their canoes. Tonty of the Iron Hand had saved them.

THE FORT ATOP THE ROCK

That night, Tonty's mind was filled with night-mares, and from time to time he shouted and struggled as if back in the grip of the Iroquois. The two priests, kneeling beside the mat where Tonty lay, had trouble keeping him from getting up and possibly breaking open the wound in his chest.

Just before dawn, Tonty's mind cleared. He had been dreaming that LaSalle, held prisoner by the Iroquois, was being burned at the stake. As Tonty awoke, he could smell the smoke.

"Save him — I've got to save him!" he cried out.

"Hush, my friend. All is well," he heard, and then he could see the faces of the priests, leaning over him. But there was no doubt about it — the air in the lodge was heavy with smoke, although the fire under the hole in the roof burned very low.

"What is burning?" Tonty asked, and tried again to rise.

Father Membre, the younger priest, said, "The

Illinois are burning their city and leaving it. But we are safe, Tonty. Etienne and the two others are standing guard through the night. Just rest, my dear friend."

Tonty tried to sleep again, but he tossed restlessly, dozing and awakening. He remembered in a waking moment that it would be only a matter of hours until the Iroquois were in the Illinois city. They would discover he had been lying about the twelve hundred approaching Illinois warriors, and the sixty well-armed Frenchmen. His mind flitted from one worry to another. He had failed LaSalle, who had counted on Tonty to advance his dream of the chain of forts in the Illinois Country. Fort Crevecoeur was gone, a charred ruin. Tonty had not even begun the new fort atop the Great Rock. The ship was unfinished — perhaps it, too, was by now a charred ruin. The valuable forge and the tools, brought from Canada with so much labor, lay at the bottom of the Illinois River. He, Tonty, had failed miserably in all that his dearest friend and respected leader had asked of him. He had not even been able to hold the workmen, so badly needed.

And LaSalle himself — what had happened to him? Why had he not returned to the Illinois Country as he had planned to do? Was he dead? Tonty, weak from loss of blood and from the shock of yesterday's attacks upon his body, drifted off again into an uneasy sleep.

Outside the lodge, Etienne Renault stood guard alone, as Jean and the other man, Pierre Leblanc, rested. Etienne saw the blood-red sun rise through a smoky haze. He shuddered at the sight of the blackened remains of what had been the largest settlement west of the Appalachian Mountains. Only a few lodges, including the one he guarded, had not been burned before the last of the Illinois Indians had moved off down the river. Etienne thought he saw a canoe being pushed away from the distant shore, just below the Great Rock, where the smoke of campfires showed the Iroquois had made camp. Soon he heard voices, calling in Iroquois langauge, and knew that the conquerors were crossing the river. He stepped inside the lodge to tell the priests what was happening.

"How is he?" he asked then, looking down at Tonty, who was lying quietly. "Shall I prepare some food for him?"

Father Membre said, "When he awakens, some good broth would help him. He will be weak for several days, and will need to let the wound in his chest heal before he is ready to travel from this horrible place."

The other priest, Father Ribourde, who was sixty-five years old and not well, said, "I wonder what the Iroquois will do with us."

"Let us hope they will listen to the Onondaga chief, and fear the power of France, and let us go free," Etienne said. "They have heard of the medicine of Tonty's iron hand. That may help. But pray, Fathers — pray for us all."

A little later, an Iroquois Indian stopped at the lodge, looked inside, and left. Before long, several braves appeared, carrying a stretcher made of poles and deerskin. Quite gently, they placed Tonty upon the stretcher. With the others following, they led the way to a rude fort, made of poles, that the Illinois had built near the river. It was somewhat charred, but had not burned.

"Iron Hand stay here," one of the Iroquois said. "You stay, too," he said to the others, and left the fort.

Tonty had awakened. "They want to watch us," he said. "I'm afraid we are Iroquois prisoners."

Tonty began to walk about a little the next day, but guards would not allow him or any of the others to go far from the fort. While they were outside, however, they noticed that there were bands of Illinois Indians in sight on the horizon, everywhere on the north side of the river.

Etienne said, "I think the warriors who were away must have returned. There seem to be many more Illinois than there were. Too bad they didn't get here three days ago."

Tonty went to speak with the Iroquois chiefs. "You see?" he said. "The Illinois are surrounding you, just as I said they would. There are two of them to each one of you."

The chiefs looked uneasy. It was clear to Tonty that they were trying to decide what to do next, not sure whether to push this war further, or to leave and come back again with a stronger force. They talked among themselves, and then asked Tonty to go with Father Membre to the Illinois camps to take a peace offer to the chiefs.

The errand was successful. The Illinois, knowing that the Iroquois were the fiercest of Indian warriors, welcomed the peace offer. They sent the son of a chief back with Tonty to discuss terms with the Iroquois chiefs. But the young man was not yet wise in the ways of treaty-makers. He was too eager to close the treaty, and the crafty old Iroquois chiefs sensed this. When the treaty was signed, they sent scouts to spy on the Illinois camps, instead of packing up and heading for their home grounds.

Tonty was again called before the Iroquois chiefs. "Where are the sixty Frenchmen hiding?" he was asked. "And we find not nearly so many Illinois warriors as you said there were. You lied, Iron Hand! You are friend to the Illinois, but not to the Iroquois!"

Tonty was sent from the council circle and kept standing to await the chiefs' decision. His chest wound pained him badly. At last he was called back.

The commanding chief said, "Illinois are like women, afraid to fight, peeking at us from over the hills but not coming to attack. We go kill their women and children and make them fight again."

This alarmed Tonty. "No, brothers, no!" he cried out. "You must not! The king, your father in France, and the governor, your brother in Canada, will be very angry with you. Your punishment will be great, and the Iroquois will disappear from the face of the land. I, too, will use my medicine against you!" With these words, Tonty held his gloved hand over his head.

The next day, the Iroquois built new canoes of elm

bark, laced onto willow limbs, getting ready to go somewhere. Two more days passed. Then the Iroquois chiefs again called Tonty and Father Membre to a council. The two Frenchmen saw that six packs of beaver skins had been tied up and were behind the commanding chief.

"They are going to make us some kind of offer," Tonty whispered to Father Membre. "Those skins are presents. To the Indian, a gift with an offer is a sign that it is made in good faith."

Tonty was right. The chief arose and began a long speech, speaking of the brotherhood of the Iroquois and the French. Then, as a pack of skins was placed before Tonty and Father Membre, he said it was a token of this friendship. A second pack was to show that the Iroquois would not go down to the Illinois camp to murder the women and children. Tonty accepted each of these gifts with speeches as polite as those of the chief.

The third pack was offered with the hope that Tonty's wounds would heal quickly. This Tonty accepted with great thanks. The fourth pack was given with a jar of oil, to give strength to both Tonty and Father Membre, as they were about to take a journey. Tonty nudged Father Membre.

"Here it comes," he whispered.

The fifth pack of furs was offered with the announcement that the sun now shone brightly upon Tonty the Great, Tonty of the Iron Hand, friend of the Iroquois. Then came the sixth and last pack. In great politeness, the chief requested that with its acceptance, Tonty and his little band would head up the Illinois River and go back home.

At last the chief's speech was ended. Tonty arose. In his best imitation of the Indian's flowery speech, he thanked the Iroquois chiefs for their gifts.

"But I cannot take them without a sign that my Iroquois brothers are also ready to go home, leaving my Illinois brothers to rebuild their city in peace," he added.

"No, no!" cried a young chief, leaping to his feet. "We shall taste the flesh of the Illinois before we go!"

Tonty scowled. His face dark with anger, he shook his gloved "medicine" hand at the chiefs. He gave each of the packs of skins a kick that thrust it toward the fire in the middle of the council circle.

Instantly, all the chiefs were on their feet and crying out against the Frenchmen. They forced Tonty and Father Membre from the lodge, and shoved them inside the little fort.

Inside, Tonty gathered his little group about him and talked to them in a low voice. "We may not live if we have one more council," he said. "I'm afraid we must give up our hope to stop the Iroquois from attacking the Illinois. We've got to get away from here."

All through the night, the Iroquois danced as the war drums beat. There was no sleep for the five men and the boy inside the fort. Tonty peered out between the poles of the flimsy palisade. He could see the shape of the Great Rock across the river, outlined against a sky in which the stars were dimming as dawn's grayness came.

"I'll be back," he said aloud. "Someday there will be a French fort atop that rock."

The gray sky in the east brightened, and soon the sun's rays were bringing a glow to the autumn hues just coming into the leaves of the trees atop the Great Rock. A messenger appeared in the entrance to the little fort. He carried word from the chief.

Tonty's eyes widened as he heard the message. All six men were invited to leave the camp, immediately.

"Well, we won't need a second invitation!" said Etienne. He stooped and began to roll up his mats and blanket. "My packing is almost finished."

The messenger led them to the river and an old, flimsy elm-bark canoe. Water began to seep into it as the first man got into it.

"It's leaking," said Etienne. "Shall we insist upon a better canoe?"

"No," said Tonty. "Let's get away from here as fast as we can, while we can. We'll bail as we go and fix the canoe later."

Etienne and Pierre paddled rapidly against the current. The others scooped out water with their hats.

When they had gone about fifteen miles up the river, the world about them seemed peaceful enough. They could risk stopping.

They need not have worried about being followed. As soon as Tonty, with the "medicine" of his iron hand, was out of sight, the chiefs began their attack on the Illinois. First they ordered the bodies in the graveyard dug up and skulls put on poles, as a sign that the Illinois city was theirs. Next, they carried out their plan of murdering the women and children in the camp down the river. They followed the Illinois braves then, as the Illinois retreated. Their victory was complete. The Illinois who escaped did not return to the land near the Great Rock for many months.

The little group of travelers on the Illinois River knew nothing of this. They spread out blankets and clothing to dry in the warm sunshine of that bright autumn afternoon, and then looked for elm trees from which to cut bark to use in canoe repairs.

Father Ribourde was not needed for this work. "I believe I'll find a spot where I can pray with my full mind and soul," he said. He walked across the sunny meadow as the others ran knife blades under lengths of elm bark and stripped bark sheets from the trees.

An hour or two later, the clothing had dried and the canoe was watertight. The sun was low in the western sky when Tonty said, "Let's go a little farther and then choose a camping place for the night. Are we all ready?"

Father Membre said, "Where is Father Ribourde?"

Tonty looked startled. "Didn't he return? He went off to pray by himself right after we stopped here. Come on, Renault. We'll go find him."

They followed the priest's path, marked by a slight bending of the meadow grasses, until they came to a grove of trees. There the tall grass ended, and the ground was nearly bare. It appeared that Father Ribourde might have knelt there.

"But where would he go from here?" Tonty wondered.

Etienne was examining the ground carefully. "Look," he said. He pointed to faint traces of moccasined feet. "I'm afraid we were all watched by some little group of Indians, and they've taken Father Ribourde with them."

They called and fired guns, but there was no answer. After going farther into the woods without seeing anything more, Tonty and Renault returned with the bad news.

"We'll camp here tonight and keep watch. If Father Ribourde is able to get back to us, the light of the fire will guide him," Tonty said. But in his heart he knew there was little hope. They stayed nearby until noon the next day. Later, they learned that Father Ribourde had been scalped by a band of Indians looking for the Iroquois.

Sadly, the men broke camp and continued their journey. Tonty decided, when they reached the Des Plaines River, to follow it northward, as the fastest route toward the western shore of Lake Michigan and the French posts at Green Bay. This was a mistake. For as Tonty and his men headed up the Des Plaines, LaSalle, with more men, was coming down the Kankakee.

LaSalle watched each day for signs of Tonty and the other men in the Illinois Country. As his loaded canoes moved into the Illinois River and traveled its waters westward and southward, LaSalle saw no sign that Tonty had come that way only a few days earlier. Hoping that Tonty would be awaiting him there, he watched eagerly for the Great Rock.

"Perhaps we shall see a new French fort atop the Rock," he said. But when it came into sight, the Rock wore only a crown of autumn-hued trees. LaSalle turned his eyes toward the meadows where the Illinois city had stood. In place of the lodges, he saw the hideous skulls on poles and the charred remains. Going onward, the men saw enough to unfold for them the story of bloody warfare. At last they came to where Fort Crevecoeur had stood. Against the dark woods, the white ribs of the unfinished ship stood like those of a great beast on its back. LaSalle found the board with the words, *Nous sommes tous sauvages.*

"Tonty, my good friend Tonty," he murmured. "Have they taken your life?" And then he saw the charred logs of Fort Crevecoeur. He had received Tonty's message and expected this, but the sight saddened him. "Fort Broken Heart — how well named it was," he thought.

But he was careful not to let the men know how worried and saddened he was. It wasn't until they reached the place where the Illinois empties into the Mississippi that the men realized how important Tonty was to LaSalle.

"And now, Sire," one of his lieutenants said to him as LaSalle looked at last upon the Great River, "shall you journey down to the Mississippi's mouth? I know that to do so has long been your dream."

LaSalle shook his head and turned away. "No. I

cannot leave my friend Tonty lost in the wilderness. We shall go back up the Illinois to watch for him. I must know what has become of him. Perhaps he is held prisoner somewhere. Next year, when I have my good lieutenant at my side, we shall make this journey again."

Winter set in by the time LaSalle was back up to the Kankakee River. He had learned nothing of what could have happened to Tonty. He and his men spent the winter at the fort they had built where the St. Joseph River emptied into Lake Michigan.

Then, one day, an Indian came to the fort, bringing news from Green Bay.

"Father Hennepin — him come back to Green Bay. Him take long journey up Great River. Then find way back to Green Bay. Now Father Hennepin gone," the Indian reported. "Him gone in great ship back to Father in France."

"I am glad to learn that Father Hennepin reached the Mississippi and is alive," said LaSalle. "But what of Tonty of the Iron Hand? Have you news of him?"

The Indian shook his head, and LaSalle was sure that Tonty was lost forever. But then the Indian went on. "Too bad, Sire. Tonty very sick. No food, and winter come. Then Potawatomi brothers find Tonty and four men with him. Iron Hand get well now. He ask about you."

LaSalle felt a heavy load drop from his shoulders. In its place, there was a new joy. Tonty was alive! The old dreams stirred again. With Tonty, LaSalle could do anything. New forts would rise — beginning with the one on the Great Rock!

"Hallo, hallo?" the men in the fort at the St. Joseph heard one spring day at dawn. They peered out the peepholes in the wall, and there was Tonty of the Iron Hand, pulling a canoe onto the beach. With him were three other men, and paddling along not far behind were more men than LaSalle could quickly count. He rushed to open the gates.

That evening, the little "spring peeper" frogs piped out their promises of warm weather on its way. Two days later, all the canoes were heading up the St. Joseph River.

"We'll forget about building a ship to sail down the Mississippi," LaSalle said. "We're not stopping this time until we have planted the flag of France on the shore at the mouth of the Great River."

On the ninth of April, 1682, LaSalle and Tonty reached the Gulf of Mexico. They planted a great column on a spot of higher ground above the marshy delta lands. On the column were the coat of arms of France, the name of Louis XIV, King of France, and the date. LaSalle announced that forever after, this land and all the land drained by the Great River and its branches, belonged to God and France. He named all this territory *Louisiana.*

"And now," he said, as he and Tonty turned back to the canoes in the river, "we shall once more begin the work of constructing a chain of forts. We'll begin at the Great Rock, my good friend. And this time we shall succeed!"

On a December day in that same year, Tonty and LaSalle stood looking down upon the Illinois River from the top of the Great Rock. Behind them, the walls of a fort were rising — a palisade of pointed log poles, fifteen feet high on the side facing the river and twenty-two feet high at the back, and eight to ten inches thick everywhere. There was only one way that men could climb up to the fort, as on three sides the cliffs were too steep.

Tonty and LaSalle watched two of the men lowering buckets tied to the ends of long ropes over the cliff. By means of them, the men hauled a water supply to the fort from the river below, each day.

"Look, Tonty," said LaSalle. He pointed down the Illinois River. "Here they come, back from the fall hunt. It is good to see the Indian town come to life again. And even better to know that with those beaver skins they bring, we shall begin a fur trade that will bring glory to France — and the money we need to build up this mighty land."

Soon afterward, LaSalle took a company of workmen with him to begin the building of more forts. A new fort arose where Fort Crevecoeur had stood, and another near the mouth of the Illinois River, on the banks of the Mississippi. Farther north, on the rivers of Wisconsin and on the upper Mississippi and to the east where the Wabash River flowed to the Ohio, others were soon being built. On the shore of Lake Michigan, a new French blockhouse marked the place where someday the great city of Chicago would begin.

When the chain of forts had been well started, LaSalle turned his thoughts to the building of the seaport city at the mouth of the Mississippi River, so that the furs gathered in the Illinois Country could be shipped to Europe by a southern route, open most of the year. In the fall of 1683, he said farewell to Tonty.

"It will be months before you see me again, Tonty,"

LaSalle explained. "I am going up to Canada and take ship for France. There I shall get more funds so that I can begin the colony at the mouth of the Mississippi. A great city will be there in a few years, my good friend!"

LaSalle explained that he would return with a ship, enter the Gulf of Mexico and follow its shores until he found the mouth of the Mississippi. There the work would begin.

Tonty of the Iron Hand stayed at Fort St. Louis, as the fort on the Great Rock was named, to manage the fur trade. Each winter, the city of lodges across the river grew larger, and spread to the meadows below the Great Rock on the southeast bank, too. Word had spread that Tonty was there to fight back the Iroquois, and that the French traders were ready to pay well for fine furs that the Indians could bring to them. One year, there were twenty thousand Indians gathered below the Great Rock. Tonty of the Iron Hand, looked up to by all the chiefs, ruled over this great settlement. Twice more the Iroquois tried to attack the Illinois tribes. Both times, led by Tonty of the Iron Hand, the Illinois beat them off until they retreated to their eastern lands.

When a year had gone by and no word had come

to Tonty of his closest friend, the man of the Iron Hand made a trip to Canada. There, too, what had happened to LaSalle remained a mystery. It was known that he had set sail from France in a good ship, but no messenger had come up the Mississippi to report his arrival there.

Tonty returned to Fort St. Louis. "I must find LaSalle," he told his lieutenant there, a man named LaForest. "Take charge here while I'm away."

With twenty-five Frenchmen and eleven Indians, Tonty headed down the Illinois River, early in 1685. Paddling through waters in which ice still floated, they went all the way down the Illinois and then to the mouth of the Mississippi. As they made their way back up the river, after finding no signs of the beginning of a fort at the river's mouth, they searched both sides of the river for many miles.

"Nothing. Absolutely no word or sign of him at all," Tonty told LaForest when at last he was back at the fort atop the Rock.

Months passed, lengthening into years. In September of 1688, three men from Arkansas came into Fort St. Louis. Tonty asked, as he did of each traveler from the south or west, "Have you any news of Sieur de LaSalle?"

Tonty had learned earlier that LaSalle's ship had reached the Gulf of Mexico, but that LaSalle had not recognized the mouth of the Mississippi as he passed it. Its much-divided delta streams did not look like the mouth of the greatest river system of North America. LaSalle had gone all the way to a bay about midway on what is now the Texas coast. There he had built a new fort that he again named Fort St. Louis. The ship's captain had left almost immediately to return to France, and LaSalle was forced to try to make his way overland from the new fort back to his other French forts. This was the last news that Tonty had received. There had been plenty of time for LaSalle to have reached the Illinois Country. He had left the Texas fort in September of 1687.

The travelers from Arkansas did have news. "Shot in the back a year ago, by one of his own men," was their reply.

Tonty recalled how this had almost happened on their first journey down the Illinois. He had been ready to kill that man, and only LaSalle's firm orders had stopped him. A terrible anger rose in him now, the stronger because he knew he would never see his dearest friend again.

"I'll get that coward!" he swore. Soon he had set

out on a journey of revenge. He heard that the man he was looking for was living with Indians in Texas. When the man with the Iron Hand, known to all the Indians of Louisiana, arrived at the Indian camp, the man was nowhere around. The Indians pretended not to know of him at all.

In sorrow, Tonty at last turned back. He must return to his duties at Fort St. Louis. Only two of his men remained with him. It was a terrible trip, for spring had come and the Mississippi Valley was badly flooded. The three men struggled northward. Unable to find food, they were forced at last to kill and eat their dogs. Before he was out of Arkansas, a fever came upon Tonty. It was September again before he reached the Great Rock.

There he remained until 1692, leaving only for short trips. In that year, the French abandoned the fort atop the Great Rock, and moved downriver to be nearer the Mississippi area. The walls of the fort began to crumble in time, but there was to be one more chapter to its history. As for Tonty, he went on to help Sieur de Bienville who later brought LaSalle's dream of a French city at the mouth of the Mississippi to reality. Both the fort atop the Great Rock and Tonty of the Iron Hand live on in legend.

PONTIAC IN THE
ILLINOIS COUNTRY

Sixty years later, there were still many log forts in the Illinois Country, with the flag of France flying over them. Little villages had grown around each of them, for French women and children had come as part of LaSalle's plan. Indians came and went freely in the villages, and many a French fur trader took an Indian girl to be his wife. There were almost always Indians camped near the villages, and the men who ran the trading posts were the busiest people in town. Indians and French usually got along well together, and life in the villages was quite peaceful. But the peace was not to last much longer.

The profitable fur trade brought traders from the British-American colonies near the Atlantic Ocean into the Ohio Country and on into the Illinois lands. Both France and England claimed this land, and they went to war over the claims in 1755. Not nearly as many French people as British people had come to live in America and the French could not defend the thousands and thousands of miles of New France. LaSalle's dream of France's glory in the New World was doomed when a treaty was signed in Paris in 1763. It gave all of France's land east of the Mississippi and in Canada to Great Britain. The land west of the Mississippi was given to Spain, in settlement of a war going on in Europe at the same time.

The war in America, that ended with the treaty, was called the French and Indian War, because the Indians joined the French, and fought against the British. Greatest of the Indian chiefs who helped France in the war was Pontiac of the Ottawas, a tribe that lived in what is now southern Michigan and northwestern Ohio. Pontiac watched the French commander at the fort at Detroit lower his flag and surrender the fort to the British. He was angry at the weakness of the French.

"Are our French brothers women instead of men? Why do they not shoot down this evil bird that drives them from their nests?" Pontiac cried out. This had been in 1760. But when Pontiac had seen that the French were not able to frighten away the British "evil birds," he had smoked the pipe of peace with the British generals.

A few months later, Pontiac again changed his

mind. After all, he reasoned, the land is neither French nor British — it belongs to the Indians. Then Pontiac set out on a long journey, calling on all the chiefs to fight for their land.

"Our hunting grounds do not belong to the English!" he cried. "We shall not stand by like women, even as the French have done. The English come into our hunting lands with their cows. They cut down our forests and plow the earth, and the good grasses are gone. Our buffalo have no feeding grounds, and they go elsewhere, leaving us without the meat we need.

"Gather around me, brothers! We shall drive the English dog back to his den by the sea! We shall drive him into the Great Sea itself, and let the waters wash over him!"

All through western Pennsylvania, where settlers from the British colonies along the coast had dared to build their little log cabins and begin to clear the land, the Indian's war cry was heard. Angry warriors, heeding Pontiac's call, stole silently through the woods to kill the pioneer as he swung his ax, and then to run to the cabin where the women and children hid in terror. Many of the settlers who escaped fled back to the safety of the settlements east of the Appalachians.

Pontiac seemed to be succeeding in driving them back to "their den by the sea," but British troops were sent to western Pennsylvania to take action against the Indians.

Pontiac brooded. He saw the British troops working under orders from one commander-in-chief. He believed that this was what the Indians must do. He would be that commander-in-chief. He sent messengers carrying red and black wampum belts to the chiefs of all the Algonkian tribes, calling them to a council. This was late in 1762.

When they had gathered, Pontiac stood before them. He raised his tomahawk high and then flung it to the ground, where its handle quivered as the blade entered the earth. Holding a war belt high, he called upon the chiefs to be ready when the moon reached a certain point the following May. They would close in upon each of the forts that the British had seized from the French, along the Great Lakes and the St. Lawrence Valley. They would prevent British troops from going farther west and south to the French forts in the Illinois Country.

When May came, in 1763, Indians were seen gathering near the forts, from Detroit on to the east. They pretended to be waiting to trade furs for the white men's whiskey, guns, and bolts of bright-colored cloth. But when the moon reached the stage Pontiac had described, they suddenly put on war paint and attacked the forts. Eight forts fell, but some, including Detroit, remained in British hands.

The French people were still living around their old trading posts. "You can band with us, brothers," Pontiac told them. "Give us guns, and we can win it all back from the British!"

But the French, because of the treaty that was signed about the same time in Paris, refused to give more guns and ammunition to the Indians to fight the British. Without supplies, Pontiac could not hold the forts he had won. His dream collapsed. The British took back the forts by blockading them until the Indians were forced to surrender.

Pontiac brooded over his losses. His scheme had failed, but he was not ready to give up. There were still forts in the Illinois Country where the British soldiers had not arrived to take command. He would go there, stop the British soldiers from reaching the forts, and the western wilderness could still be saved for the Indian. . . .

On a warm day in July, 1764, there was scarcely a

sound to be heard in Kaskaskia, the largest of the French fort settlements on the Mississippi. Most of the people were resting through the warmest hours of the afternoon. Earlier in the day, a few had gone to the fields outside the village, where all had their long, narrow strips of farming land, to do a bit of hoeing. The women had tended the gardens behind their houses in the cool hours, too, pouring a bit of water here and there where a treasured flower drooped in the summer heat, and pulling a clump of grass from the fertile valley soil where it was crowding in on the beans. Now all the people were resting. Some were lying down inside the houses. Others leaned back in their chairs on the broad, shady front porches.

No one heard the first sounds of horses' hoofs that reached the village that afternoon. Even up in Fort Chartres, on the bluff overlooking the village and the Mississippi River, no one was alert enough to notice the cloud of dust that marked the coming of a group of horses on the trail that led into Kaskaskia from the east. There was seldom any need for keeping a close watch.

Commander Neyon, in charge of the handful of soldiers in the fort and of the militia company of the French village, was expecting a company of British soldiers to come to take command. None of the fighting in the war had been done this far west. He hated to see the British flag go up over Kaskaskia, but on the other hand, he would be glad to leave this sleepy, peaceful little post.

But suddenly Kaskaskia was no longer peaceful. Someone heard the sound of the horses' hoofs, and looked down the street.

"A war party!" he cried. "Indians!"

People rushed outside to see. Some ran back into the houses in fright. For there, riding into town, was a whole company of fierce-looking chiefs and warriors, of tribes unknown to the western Illinois Country. Leading them, in full war dress and paint, was Chief Pontiac. Seeing the terror of the people, Pontiac held up a belt of white wampum. He did not stop in the village. His horsemen turned onto the road that circled around behind the bluff, and climbed toward the fort.

Commander Neyon had his men lined up in readiness for the arrival of the chiefs. After hasty greetings, he said, "Now, Chief Pontiac, surely you have given up your plan to make war again. You must have come to your senses after what happened last year."

A steely glint came into Pontiac's eyes, and he drew

himself as tall as he could. With great dignity, he signaled his chiefs to bring forth a black and red wampum belt. He laid it before Commander Neyon and said, "My brother, this is the answer I give you. I came to invite you and all my French brothers to go with me in war against the English."

Neyon sighed. He was going to have more trouble. "Chief Pontiac, you are my brother," he said. "But surely you know that now the French and English are also brothers. We have smoked the calumet together and exchanged belts of white wampum. I cannot take up the hatchet against my brothers.

"You must know now that we all live under the Great Father in England. He is your father now, and the English are your brothers."

Pontiac's eyes blazed. "The English are not my brothers. They steal my hunting grounds. They drive away the buffalo that feed my people. True brothers do not do that. Take up the hatchet with us, and together we will drive away the evil bird and have this land for our own!"

Neyon grew angry. "Didn't you hear what I said? I am not interested in taking up any hatchets." He kicked the war belt back to Pontiac.

The great chief folded his arms across his chest. One

of his chiefs stooped and picked up the war belt. There was silence for a long minute, and Neyon plucked at his moustache nervously.

When Pontiac spoke, his tones were quiet. "Brother, you have listened to the whistling of the evil birds and believed their false notes," he said. "We shall sorrow to see those birds pick at your flesh." He turned and started toward the gate of the fort. But, before he left, he turned back and requested a keg of rum.

"Just like an Indian," Neyon thought, and ordered the keg of rum. When he had given it to Pontiac, he watched the Indians leave. "We don't need to worry, men," he said. "They'll get so drunk on rum that they'll forget their big ideas."

Pontiac and his men rode northward from the village toward a large Indian camp. The Kaskaskians could hear the sounds of drums and war songs throughout the night that followed. Many of them shivered as they turned in their beds, trying to sleep.

The great chief was not seen again in Kaskaskia until the leaves had turned to the colors of war paint. But the French people of Kaskaskia often gathered in little groups to tell of what they had seen and to share their worries over what was about to happen. Small groups of chiefs had come to the fort again and again, asking for guns and ammunition. They wanted only guns and gunpowder and lead from the fur traders' shelves when they came with furs.

"We'll give them all the ammunition they want," the fur traders said. "As soon as the British come in here, you can be sure they'll take all our business away. If we can help the Indians keep the British away, our trade will go on."

"Sure, we'll help you," one of the traders told the Indians, when an Indian spoke of wanting his French brother's help. "Look here." The trader took a folded paper, decorated with a seal and ribbons, from the shelf where he had kept it for just such a moment. "Here is a letter from the king of France. He says you should all do as Pontiac says. You pass the word along to all the chiefs that your father in France wants them to do as Pontiac says and that he will help them."

When the Indians had gone, an astonished villager asked to see the letter. The fur trader laughed. "Did I fool you, too?" he asked. "I wrote that letter myself. A man has to do what he can to keep his business alive."

In the meantime, Chief Pontiac had journeyed back to his home village on the Maumee River, near the present city of Toledo, Ohio, to gather a company of braves from among his own people. Then he started again for the Illinois Country, stopping at every Indian camp and village along the way to speak before the chiefs and braves. His great voice rose time and again in pleas for all Indians to work together to save the land for themselves. Each tribe agreed to send its warriors in answer to the chief's call.

In the fort at Kaskaskia, there was now a new commander, named St. Ange. Commander St. Ange was as anxious as Neyon had been to have the British troops arrive to take over Fort Chartres. Troops had been sent by way of the Ohio River, only to be turned back by Indian attacks. Then the British had been put on board ships and taken to New Orleans. The latest word Commander St. Ange had received was that the troops had started up the Mississippi, on a keelboat, from New Orleans.

One day news came to the commander about the British soldiers. He read the message and a look of anger came over his face. One of his lieutenants asked, "Have they been delayed again, Commander?"

"Delayed? They've turned back again! We'll sit here until we rot!" the commander fumed. "It's the work of that crazy Indian, Pontiac! Seems he had men on both banks of the river watching for the redcoats. They were fired at with deadly arrows no matter which bank they went near, and out in the middle they couldn't move the boat against the current. So they went back."

The lieutenant, who rather liked his life at Fort Chartres, turned away to hide a grin. He could just picture the faces of those stiff-backed British soldiers when they came floating back to New Orleans. They must have been as red as their coats! He learned later that his guess had been true. The French in New Orleans had laughed and jeered so heartily that the British soldiers had soon departed for the British fort at Pensacola, Florida.

St. Ange was expecting word of a new attempt at sending troops when, instead, he heard the whooping and shouting of Indians. He went to the fort gateway, and his heart sank at what he saw.

At the head of as wild a looking band as St. Ange had ever seen was Chief Pontiac, riding his spirited horse. His back was straight. His head was held high. Tufts of feathers crowned his greased black hair. His body shone with the grease of red war paint. Behind him was a great body of equally fierce-looking warriors.

"Must be four hundred of them," the commander said.

Pontiac dismounted and, with a group of chiefs behind him, stood before Commander St. Ange. The commander had never seen a wampum belt anything like the one that Pontiac ordered placed at his feet. It was six-feet long and four-inches wide, all worked in the designs of forty-seven tribes, in shells died red and black, the colors of war. Pontiac's work had resulted in forty-seven tribes agreeing to join in his plan to stop the British troops and settlers from advancing any farther to the west.

Pontiac's tones were polite as he greeted St. Ange. He said, "Brother, we have long wished to see you, and to shake hands with you in the fashion of our white brothers. We want you to show us that you are our true brother by smoking the calumet with us. We wish to bring to your mind the many battles in which we fought side by side against the English dogs. I love the French. I have come here with my warriors to make a war that will bring justice to both my French and Indian brothers."

St. Ange listened as Pontiac went on, speaking of the ammunition, guns and troops he expected the French to supply. The commander did not know what kind of answer he should give. He was bound by a treaty with the English. Yet he did not dare bring the anger of Pontiac and his great war party upon the helpless people of the French villages.

"If only the British troops had arrived," he thought. If St. Ange had only known it, British troops were nowhere near Kaskaskia. A second company had been sent to New Orleans, but as soon as they learned of Chief Pontiac's band of warriors, they had turned back.

St. Ange had to make a reply of some kind. He gave greetings to his "brothers," and agreed that they had stood side by side through the years and that he valued that relationship.

"But I must tell you the truth, Chief Pontiac. My warehouses are almost empty. We expected the British soldiers here before now, as you well know. We have therefore allowed our supplies to be used without replacing them. I cannot fill your request."

It was clear that Pontiac did not believe the commander's reason for not giving the Indians the arms they asked for. He had his chiefs pick up the great war belt, and saying he would return, led his men away. They made camp at the edge of the village and there they settled down for the winter. Other Indians

arrived to join them, waiting the coming of spring when the great war would begin.

Usually, the people of the French villages livened up the winter evenings with dancing and parties, but the winter of 1764-1765 was long and cold and spirits were heavy. The Indians, camping all around the villages, grew restless as the weeks went by. The traders' shelves were empty, and each day it became harder to handle the Indians who came to the posts. Just as trouble seemed sure to come, a boatload of goods came up the river from New Orleans. The traders' shelves were filled again, and the Indians became more cheerful.

Pontiac watched the fort for signs that Commander St. Ange was getting ready to help him in his new war. He saw none. But he learned from new Indian arrivals that the English had been busy. They had sent the old trader, George Croghan, who knew Indians well and was liked by many of them, to warn the Indians not to take part in Pontiac's war. Croghan told them that they would be punished if they did not let the boats with soldiers and supplies go down the Ohio in peace.

"English send boats full of presents for us, too,"

other chiefs told Pontiac. "Maybe best if we smoke calumet with them."

"No!" cried Pontiac. "Do you not see that they want to quiet us so that they can seize all our hunting grounds? They will push us farther and farther west until we fall into the western sea! Do not listen to the English dogs!"

But the loads of presents the English sent down-river with Croghan spoke louder than Pontiac's cries. The tribes in the eastern part of the Illinois Country gathered at the old French fort at Vincennes, on the Wabash River in Indiana, to sign peace treaties with the British. Pontiac decided he would have to change his plans.

Knowing he could not win without the help of the tribes of the eastern Illinois Country, Pontiac called the chiefs gathered at Kaskaskia into council.

"Our brothers in the East have listened to the whistling of the evil birds, and our brothers the French are women who will not fight," he told them. "We are not ready to push the English dogs into the sea alone, nor shall we sit here idly and let them come here to spring upon us. We shall go to meet their messenger, Trader Croghan, and smoke the calumet with him. We shall tell him that we are joyful to be in the sunshine of peace.

"We will go to the Englishman and take his hand. Then, when he has broken his promises, as he always does, we will be stronger. We shall have all our brothers gathered behind us, and we will let the hatchet fall upon the English heads and split them wide."

So Pontiac went to Vincennes to meet Trader Croghan. Great councils were held there, with long speeches by both Croghan and Pontiac. Promises were made, and many belts of wampum were exchanged. Croghan presented his last one with the words, "Children, with this belt I take the hatchet out of your hands, and pluck up a large tree, and bury it deep, so that it may never be found any more. I plant the tree of peace, which all our children may sit under, and smoke in peace with their fathers."

A few days later, Croghan, well satisfied with what he had done, headed back toward Fort Pitt. He met a company of one hundred Scotch Highlander soldiers of the British army, coming down the river. They were heading for Fort Chartres, and reached Kaskaskia just as the snows of another winter began to fall.

The French flag was lowered. LaSalle's dream of

the glory of France was truly ended. Pontiac alone dreamed of taking the land from the British. He was bitter as he saw the treaties broken and the British-American settlers pushing farther and farther into the lands west of the Appalachians, returning to their cabins in western Pennsylvania and talking of settling in the Ohio Country. By April, 1769, Pontiac was once more ready to gather the Indian tribes, with proof that the English treaties meant little.

He laid his plans carefully. This time he must not fail. He must be wise in all he said and did. His first step was to go to the Mississippi Valley to check conditions there. He visited the fort at Kaskaskia once again. A day or two after his arrival, he put on a military uniform given to him by the French General Montcalm in the French and Indian War. In full dress and full dignity, he crossed the Mississippi River and went north to the new town of St. Louis, which had been begun by the French just at the time that the treaties were being signed to end the French and Indian War. Although the land was officially Spanish, St. Louis was still French in spirit.

In St. Louis, Pontiac was treated as an honored guest by St. Ange, the man who had been commander at Fort Chartres, and by Pierre LaClede and the young Chouteau brothers, leading fur traders and founders of St. Louis. But after two or three days, Chief Pontiac told young Pierre Chouteau that he must go back across the river.

"My brothers gather in great numbers at Cahokia," he told the trader. "They await my coming to lead them."

Cahokia was almost directly across the Mississippi from St. Louis. There the tribes had gathered in answer to a call Pontiac had sent out. There were Potawatomi, Kickapoo, Sac and Fox and a scattering of others. The Illinois were there, too, but they were now a weak tribe, looked down upon by many of the other Algonkians. But all of them joined in a great feast to welcome Pontiac.

When the feasting ended, Pontiac went alone to complete his business at Kaskaskia. As he left Cahokia, one of the English traders there, a man named Williamson, watched him start down the trail through the woods. He signaled an Illinois Indian to come close.

"Look," he said, "that old chief is here for no good. He wants to make trouble for all of us. Now, you want to keep on getting all the things I have for you at my post, don't you? You stop Pontiac and keep him from starting trouble again."

The Indian grunted. "What you pay me to stop him?" he asked.

Williamson said, "Here. A whole barrel of rum is set aside for you. And something else when the old chief is dead."

The bargain was sealed. The Indian followed Pontiac into the woods. The next day, the great chief lay dead on the trail.

Word quickly spread that an Illinois Indian had killed Pontiac. Among the warriors gathered at Cahokia, anger was great against all Illinois Indians for what one of their number had done. The Potawatomi, eager to avenge the death of Pontiac, went on the warpath. They did not even stop to bury the old chief.

The weak Illinois retreated. Through the months that followed, the Potawatomi tracked them down wherever they hid. Legend says that some of the Illinois went to the Great Rock, where once Tonty had ruled over their fathers. The Illinois fought from atop the rock, where the log walls of the fort were now in ruins. When the Illinois lowered ropes to get buckets of water, the Potawatomi cut the ropes, and they blocked the pathway that led to the top of the Great Rock. The Illinois starved up there, while the Potawatomi camped where once the great Illinois towns had stood.

Today, thousands of people visit the Great Rock each year, and gaze out over the river and the meadows and rolling land as LaSalle and Tonty once did. Because of the Illinois Indians who were held there by the Potawatomi, they call the place Starved Rock.

As for Pontiac, his body lay on the trail between the two French forts until St. Ange sent men to bring it back to St. Louis. He and the Chouteaus buried the great chief with honors, near the church that faced the Mississippi River.

When their city was two hundred years old, in 1964, the people of St. Louis began to build a great arch on the riverfront. Thousands of people now visit the Gateway Arch each year. Chief Pontiac whose hopes died in the old French forts of the Illinois Country, just as LaSalle's did, lies somewhere near the foot of the great arch.

GUNPOWDER TO WIN
THE WEST

What Pontiac had feared was coming true. Six years after his death, the English-Americans were moving into the lands west of the mountains to stay, and the sound of the ax was heard in the heart of Kentucky.

One day in 1775, a young boy sat alone in the Kentucky woods, turning a stick over a campfire. His eyes were on the sizzling wild duck that he had run the stick through, and he did not see the tall, red-haired young man who stood only a few feet away at the edge of the small clearing.

"That smells good to a hungry man," the watcher said, and the boy dropped the duck into the fire. "Indians!" the boy thought, and was ready to run until he realized the words had not been spoken as an Indian would speak them. He turned and saw a big man who clearly could not be an Indian, even though he was dressed in deerskin. Who ever saw an Indian with carrot-red hair?

"My name is Clark — George Rogers Clark," the

newcomer said. "Don't let that duck burn, please."

The boy, who was fifteen years old but small for his age, rescued the duck. "Mine is James Ray," he said as he brushed the ashes from the duck. "What brings you here, Mr. Clark? Ain't nobody in all these parts except us folks at Harrod's."

"That's just where I'm going," said Clark. "I've been doing some surveying farther up the Ohio for the Ohio Land Company for two or three years now. Then I heard that William and James Harrod were out here in this Kentucky wilderness. I came to see how you brave fellows were doing, and to see if I could do anything to help you."

James looked up from the duck, which he was now removing from the stick. He saw that his visitor was eyeing it hungrily.

"Can I share it with you, Mr. Clark?" he asked politely. He held the little fowl toward his visitor. "Help yourself."

George Rogers Clark did exactly that. James, hungry from a day of hunting in the woods to get meat for the people of Harrodsburg, watched his delicious bit of food disappear. There was only a little meat left on the bones when at last the guest handed the duck back to James.

"I'm sorry, James," Clark said. "I didn't leave much for you, did I?"

"It will hold me until we get to the fort," James said. He was too polite to tell this tall stranger how hungry he really was. When he had gnawed off every last scrap that was left on the duck's bones, James put out his fire. He picked up a deerskin in which were the choice roasting pieces of meat that he was taking to Harrodsburg.

"I'll carry that," Clark said. "Lead on, James."

Soon they could hear the ringing of axes, where the first settlers in Kentucky were building cabins and setting up pointed poles to make a palisaded fort. They had come down the Ohio in March, a year earlier, led by James Harrod who had found this land that he liked when he had come on a hunting trip into Kentucky. He had brought his settlers by boat, from the Ohio up the Kentucky River and they had begun their settlement. But that summer of 1774, another hunter, named Daniel Boone, had come to the little cabins in the wilderness to warn Harrod and his people that Indians were on the warpath. All had gone back east for the fall and winter. But now they were back, building palisaded walls between the cabins to make a fort, and adding more cabins. They would stay, they said, even if Indian attacks came.

James Harrod met the newcomer as young James Ray brought Clark into the settlement.

"You are more than welcome, Mr. Clark," said Harrod. "Stay with us as long as you like. We hope you will decide that Harrodsburg is your home."

For the next year, Harrodsburg came as close as any place to being "home" to George Rogers Clark, whose family was back in the foothills of North Carolina. All that summer, he came back often to Harrodsburg from his trips to survey more land for the Ohio Company. He had fallen in love with this western land, since his first trip into it in 1772. He hoped soon to go to see the Illinois Country that the traders had told him about, where open prairie lands stood ready for the settler's plow. But during the summer of 1775, he was kept busy in Kentucky.

He went to see the new settlement at Boonesborough, just being built. About the same time that Harrod had been bringing his people back to Kentucky by way of the Ohio and Kentucky Rivers, Daniel Boone and a group of other frontiersmen had cut trees and blazed an overland trail to Kentucky. Called the Wilderness Road, it marked a route settlers could follow from Cumberland Gap, a mountain pass at the place where the present states of Kentucky, Virginia, and Tennessee meet. Boone's own family and those of some of his friends and relatives were coming to live at Boonesborough, the new settlement at the end of the trail.

But there was a problem that disturbed George Rogers Clark. He told James Harrod about it. "We have trouble on our hands," he said. "You are counting on getting title to this land from the colony of Virginia, and I am surveying more land for the Ohio Company of Virginia, in the belief that Virginia owns this land and has the right to make treaties with the Indians and to sell land grants here."

"That is right," said James Harrod.

George went on. "Now, here's the problem. I talked to this fellow, Daniel Boone, who is building Boonesborough. He got title to the land, not from the Virginia government, but from Judge Richard Henderson of Carolina. Seems this Judge Henderson made a treaty with the Cherokee Indians and paid them for this land, after deciding it was really theirs. He formed the Transylvania Company and sent Boone to lead settlers to Kentucky, which he calls Transylvania, and says he owns. Claims that Harrodsburg is in Transylvania, too, and only he can sell you this land. Now, somebody is going to be left without clear land titles, and it will be the hard-working settlers who are building cabins and clearing the land that will be left with nothing to show for their work, either here or over in Boonesborough."

"I don't want to lose title to this land," said Harrod. "What can we do about it, Clark?"

"The way to settle it is to get Virginia to make Kentucky a county, with elected representatives from here to the House of Burgesses," said Clark. "I'm going back to Williamsburg to see the governor."

As the summer ended, George Rogers Clark was in Williamsburg. There he learned of all that had been taking place in the colonies along the coast since April of 1775. He learned of the Battles of Lexington and Concord and Bunker Hill in Massachusetts, and of how George Washington of Virginia had been made commander of armies from all the colonies. He heard discussions about whether the colonies should separate from England altogether and form a new country, or just fight for more rights in government. People told him of how Patrick Henry had excited everyone with his fiery words, "Give me liberty, or give me death!"

"That's the way I feel about it, too," George told

the people back in Kentucky.

In 1776, Virginia made Kentucky a county of that state, after the Declaration of Independence had been signed, and the new nation, the United States of America had begun its life. That fall, George Rogers Clark and a young lawyer, John Gabriel Jones, were sent to Williamsburg to represent Kentucky. They found that Patrick Henry had been elected governor of the state. Lawyer Jones went to visit his family while Clark went to see Governor Henry. The governor had been ill, and was at his home in the country.

George had serious matters on his mind. "Governor Henry, what are we going to do to make sure that Kentucky and all the rest of that land, away out to the Mississippi River, is taken away from the British? There are British soldiers out there in all the old French forts. Are you sending soldiers out to capture the forts from them?"

Patrick Henry's mouth tightened in his lean face, and his eyes were like flint as he looked at young Clark. "Have you any idea, sir," he said after a moment, "of what problems we have in getting enough men for a fighting force to drive the British from so important a place as New York City? General Washington needs every man we can send him, and more."

His face softened as he saw the stricken look in Clark's eyes. "But I agree with you, Clark. The frontier lands should be part of the United States when we have ended this struggle. You have my approval to organize the men on the frontier to defend themselves," he said. He took pen and ink and busied himself at his desk. In a few minutes, he handed Clark a paper. "You will have to sell the Executive Council of Virginia on the idea, however. Here is a letter to take to Williamsburg. It requests that you be granted some ammunition, and be commissioned a major in the Virginia militia."

George took the letter. Soon he was on his way to meet with the council. As he rode toward Williamsburg, his thoughts went to those French forts and how they could be seized from the British. It seemed that if it was to be done, he — George Rogers Clark — must be the one to plan it.

The council agreed to allow Clark to organize a militia and to give him the five hundred pounds of gunpowder he asked for.

"But you'll have to move it to Kentucky yourself. We can't pay for transportation," he was told.

Clark's hopes, building higher each moment as he

planned his work, crashed to the ground. He had no money to pay wagoners and boatmen to take the barrels of gunpowder to Kentucky. His temper got the better of him. "Keep your gunpowder!" he shouted. "If a country is not worth protecting, it is not worth claiming. Mark my words — if Virginia doesn't consider all that land worth having, someone else will!" He slapped the flat side of his sword down on the tabletop, and the ring of the metal was all that was heard for a moment. Then Clark sheathed his sword and turned on his heel. "Good-bye, gentlemen," he said, and left the room.

He was soon riding away from Williamsburg. His anger had not died when, after he had traveled about thirty miles, he heard the galloping hoofs of a horse behind him. "Mr. Clark!" the rider called, and reined up alongside George's horse. "The council asks you to return. They have a new offer to make you."

Clark went back. This time, the council offered to get the powder up to Fort Pitt at Virginia's expense. Since this part of the trip was the most difficult and expensive, Clark felt that he could see that the powder went the rest of the way to Kentucky. He would have it loaded onto a flatboat and float it down the Ohio River.

Lawyer Jones arrived just as Clark was ready to leave Williamsburg. Together, they went to Pittsburgh.

"Our problem now will be to get that gunpowder safely past the Indians," Clark told him. "I have been told that the British government pays them well for anything they can do to help them fight against us."

They found a flatboat and seven men to help get the precious cargo down the Ohio. They were near the end of the trip, about two days from the mouth of the Kentucky River, when Clark saw Indians watching from the Ohio shore.

"They're following us, waiting until we get the gunpowder to a handy place for them," he said. He called the crew together and told them of his plan to save the gunpowder.

"Tonight we'll unload it onto land, under cover of darkness," he said."We'll hide the barrels and get men from the forts to come and take it the rest of the way overland. A few men can take care of hiding the barrels while the rest of us float on down the river, just as if the barrels were still in the cargo box."

That night the men quietly unloaded the twenty-five kegs, each holding twenty pounds of gunpowder. At dawn, the flatboat shoved off from shore, just as was usual after a night's rest. One of the men who stayed on shore was Lawyer Jones. He went to find a company of soldiers and surveyors the men had seen a few days earlier. Jones told them of the need to carry the kegs to the forts. On the way back to the hiding place, Shawnee Indians attacked the party. Jones was one of three men who lost their lives. Four were captured by the Indians and the rest escaped, giving up the attempt to get the gunpowder.

A few days later, the men who escaped made their way to one of the forts. Terror was spreading through the tiny settlements, as word spread of more Indian raids. At Harrodsburg, Major Clark was busy training men. He said, "We've got to get that gunpowder." James Harrod offered to lead a party to get it. Simon Kenton, one of the men who knew the woods and Indians best, went along as a scout.

They found the hidden kegs, and strapped them onto the horses' backs, four to each packhorse and one behind the saddle of each rider. With Kenton keeping watch ahead of them, they followed a narrow trail along the river's edge until they came to a buffalo trace that Kenton knew well. Since the Shawnee were taking their captives back to the Ohio villages, Kenton felt that the open trail was best so that the trip could be made as rapidly as possible.

They reached Harrodsburg without meeting an Indian.

"Now we can begin," said Major Clark. But he did not tell anyone his plans. If the men of Kentucky knew that it was in Clark's mind to lead them all the way to the French forts on the Mississippi River, they might have deserted. How could a handful of frontiersmen attack the trained soldiers of the British army, secure behind the log walls of the Illinois Country forts?

STARS AND STRIPES
OVER THE FRENCH FORTS

George Rogers Clark laid his plans carefully. The year 1777 had begun when the gunpowder was safely stored at Harrodsburg. The next step was to organize the frontier men as members of the militia of the new county. By March, he had every man who could handle a rifle enrolled.

And none too soon. That was the month that Chief Blackfish led his Shawnee to Harrodsburg. James Ray, out hunting, barely escaped with his life, and his brother William was killed. Harrodsburg, with its supply of gunpowder, held off the attackers. The raids continued, with one little fort after another being hit. The year 1777 was called the bloody year.

"We can't just sit here and wait. We'll lose Kentucky and all the land to the Mississippi to the British if we do," decided George Rogers Clark, right after the Harrodsburg attack.

He sent two men, Ben Linn and Sam Moore, to scout the land between Kentucky and the Illinois

Country forts. In a few weeks they were back.

"We pretended we were hunters, and walked into Kaskaskia," Sam said when he and Ben were alone with Clark. "We told the people we wanted some supplies before we went trapping. Fellow named Bentley, who had a store there, seemed real anxious to help us."

Clark nodded. "I know of Bentley," he said. "But what about the French people? And how many soldiers are in the fort?"

"There weren't many British soldiers there," Ben Linn said. "They haven't even got a British commander in the fort. A Frenchman named Rocheblave was there. He seemed to be counting on the militia in the town to protect the place."

"It didn't seem like the British cared to bother much with those French forts away out there on the Mississippi, except for a few traders like Bentley," Moore added. "The people all spoke French."

Ben said, "Bentley told us that the Indians knew we were from Kentucky. He warned us that we'd better get out of town before they held a council and decided to take us prisoners."

Clark asked, "How did the Indians know you weren't British?"

Sam Moore was fingering his light-colored felt hat. "Seems this kind of hat that most of us wear here in Kentucky isn't seen in the Illinois Country."

Clark tucked this bit of information away. He would see that his Kentuckians didn't give themselves away so easily in the future.

Ben Linn had one more thing to add to the report. "Bentley said the French people there don't like the British, but they are afraid of Americans. They've been hearing about such things as the Boston Tea Party, and they think we are all a wild lot, not civilized." Looking at his be-whiskered, deerskin-clad messengers, Clark could see how Kentuckians would do little to change this idea.

"So much the better," he thought. "If they are afraid of us, we may win the forts more easily."

Clark had his charts and plans ready when he went again to see Governor Patrick Henry. It was fall by then, and news had just come of American victories in New York.

"Yes, we can send some men to the West with you now," the governor said. "Not the thousand you've asked for, but you may raise a company or two in Pittsburgh."

A company was about one hundred men. When

Clark left Pittsburgh in May, 1778, he had a new commission as lieutenant colonel. On Colonel Clark's flatboats were about 150 new soldiers for his fighting force and twenty new settlers for Kentucky, traveling with the soldiers. They were met by Simon Kenton and some other Kentuckians at the mouth of the Kentucky River, and went on downriver to new headquarters at Corn Island. The new settlers began their clearings on the south bank of the Ohio across from the island. It became Louisville. Corn Island has since been washed away by floodwaters of the Ohio River.

Clark trained his new men for a few weeks, and then he knew he had to tell them what they were going to do.

"Attack the British forts? A thousand miles from here? Colonel, that's through enemy country all the way!" Clark's officers were shocked at the idea. As for the new soldiers, some of them decided they'd rather desert. Led by a lieutenant, some of them waded and swam to the Kentucky shore one night and disappeared into the woods. Clark sent men after them, but only seven or eight were brought back.

But on the morning of June 24, 1778, Clark started out with 178 men, including as many Kentuckians as could be spared from the work of protecting the Kentucky forts. A number of Kentuckians, Daniel Boone among them, were in Ohio or the fort at Detroit, held prisoner by Indians or by the British Commander, General Henry Hamilton, whose head-quarters were at Detroit.

Clark said to his officers, "We'll go down the Ohio to Fort Massac, hide our boats there and store some of our supplies. Then we'll march overland to Kaskaskia." Fort Massac was just across from today's Paducah, Kentucky.

Captain Leonard Helm, a Kentuckian who had been an Indian fighter for many years, said, "We can get there quicker by boat, Colonel. Why don't we just head right up the Mississippi and get on with it?"

"Because they would see us coming," Clark said. "They would know that we are just a handful of men, and would hold out in Fort Chartres until help came. No, Leonard, we've got to take them by surprise, and the only way to do it is to go overland and keep out of sight when we get close."

Just before they got to Fort Massac, a canoe with one man in it came swiftly down the Ohio. The men recognized one of the men from Louisville.

"Colonel Clark, I have a message for you that

came from Fort Pitt after you left," the man said. He handed an official-looking paper to Clark.

Clark's eyes lighted as he read it. France had signed an agreement to help the Americans in their war against Great Britain! This was just what he needed to get the French people in the villages to help him.

On July 4, 1779, Commander Rocheblave had no idea that about 180 Americans who were armed with long rifles, tomahawks and hunting knives were less than a day's march south of Kaskaskia. If he had known, he would not have left the town to go down the Mississippi to meet with the Spanish governor across the river at New Madrid. It was suppertime when he got back to his house inside Fort Chartres. This was not the same fort that Pontiac had visited on the bluff above town less than ten years earlier. A new fort had been built close to the bank of the Kaskaskia River, just above the joining of the Kaskaskia with the Mississippi.

After supper, Rocheblave sat down at his desk, took quill and ink bottle and a sheet of paper and penned a letter to General Hamilton. He wrote, "It is my duty to report to you that a strong force of Americans has been seen recently descending the Ohio River." He added that he believed the boats had gone on down the Mississippi. He sealed the folded sheet with wax and arose.

"It has been a long day, my dear," he said to Mme. Rocheblave. "I am very tired. Let us retire."

As the commander climbed the stairs to his bedroom in the last light of that long July evening, George Rogers Clark stood not far away, on the opposite bank of the Kaskaskia. He was looking over the town. Was the quiet just a trap to lure the men into it? Had they been seen as they crossed the prairies that afternoon? If so, there was no sign.

Some say that Bentley, the trader, had boats ready for Clark's men, tied up near a little log farmhouse on the east bank of the Kaskaskia, a mile or so above the town. The farmer who lived there seemed to want to be helpful. When Clark returned to the farmyard, where his men were resting, he spoke to the farmer.

"Where are the Indians?" he asked.

"Not many are there now," the farmer answered. Just then a faint sound of music and voices drifted up the river.

"What's that?" Clark asked.

The farmer said, "Just some of the townsfolk livening up the evening a bit with some dancing, as they often do."

Clark lined up his men and divided them into three groups. The smallest group was made up of a few of his old friends from Kentucky, including Simon Kenton.

"You men move in and take positions around the town, but don't make a sound until you get my signal from the fort," he said to the largest group. To the second group he said, "These fellows will set up a great racket when they get the signal, to make it sound like there are a thousand of us. Then you boys move in to help them get the townspeople under control. Make them so scared they won't dare try any tricks. Let's hope that most of the militia are at that dance, and have left their guns at home. You boys," and Clark turned to the little band of bearded, dirty Kentuckians, "are going into the fort with me."

The Kentuckians grinned. That was to their liking.

Silently the men crossed the river and advanced to the town itself. While some moved cautiously along the streets, and the reserves waited at the edge of the town, Clark and his Kentuckians went up to the gates of the fort. No guards were seen. In a few minutes they were inside. Rocheblave's house was dark.

A few minutes later, Rocheblave felt a rough hand on his shoulder. Madame Rocheblave screamed, for on her side of the bed a giant of a man stood pointing a rifle at her. In the light of candles, held by other fierce-looking men, she saw that the man had long red hair and a red beard. "Quiet, madame. I'll not harm you," Simon Kenton, her captor, said, and Madame Rocheblave pulled the covers up and over her head.

On the other side of the bed, another red-haired, red-bearded giant said, "Surrender, in the name of the United States of America."

Rocheblave could only sputter. He was pulled from the bed. Clark allowed him to put his robe over his nightshirt, and then marched him down the stairs.

"You may continue your sleep, Madame," he said, as he left. All the soldiers followed Clark downstairs, closing the bedroom door behind them. It is quite certain that Madame Rocheblave did not go back to sleep, for just then the signal shots were fired from the fort and a great noise arose in the town, with screams from the French people and shouts from the soldiers who had taken them by surprise.

And so, Kaskaskia was won. The next day, fifty miles up the Mississippi, Cahokia also was taken without a shot being fired, with the aid of a French priest who went ahead to tell the people they would not be hurt if they surrendered quietly. When he had everything under control, Clark gave out the news that the French were now allies of the Americans. This helped a great deal, and soon life was getting back to normal among the French people.

"Now," said Clark, "before word gets up to Hamilton at Detroit about all this, let's get on to Vincennes, over on the Wabash River. Then we'll have all of the Illinois Country."

"I'm ready," said Simon Kenton. Soon he and two other men were on their way to Vincennes as spies. They wrapped themselves in blankets, to look like Indians, and walked about the streets of the village. They watched the fort, Fort Sackville, to see if there were many British soldiers.

"It should be easy to take Vincennes," they reported to Clark when they returned.

Again a French priest went ahead to tell the people that the Americans and French were now working together against the British. Then Captain Leonard Helm took twenty-five men and with no trouble moved into the fort. After a while, some of the twenty-five men left Vincennes to go back to Kentucky.

"They need us more at home than you do here, Captain Helm," they said. Their short enlistment terms had ended.

While Helm went to Vincennes, Clark was busy convincing a gathering of Indians at Cahokia that the Americans were friends of the French people, and that the Indians should not attack them. When he returned to Kaskaskia, there was bad news. General Hamilton had heard of the capture of the three forts and had led eighty British soldiers and a large company of Indians to Vincennes. Helm could do nothing. He was now a prisoner inside Fort Sackville.

A British spy was caught near Cahokia, and from him Hamilton's plans were learned. "He knows that you have only eighty men left at Kaskaskia," Clark was told. "He has settled down at Vincennes for the winter, but he intends to drive you out in the spring."

"It will be all over for us in the spring when he comes," Clark thought.

"We just won't let it end that way!" he said. "Surprise worked for us before. We'll try it again."

This was the end of January, 1779. Hamilton would not expect men to be on the march for another six weeks. There was just time to try a surprise attack. He sent a messenger to Cahokia to round up all the French militia who would come, and ordered the Kaskaskia militia to get ready to march to save their French brothers in Vincennes.

On February 4, a keelboat, hastily fitted with six small cannons, was loaded with supplies and started down the Mississippi, commanded by George's cousin, John Rogers. The boat would turn up the Ohio River and then into the Wabash. It would meet the main body of men just below Vincennes, which was about ninety miles up the Wabash River.

"You should be there by the time we make the overland march, John," George said as Rogers was ready to leave. "Hide the boat in the thickets and watch for us. Good luck!"

The next day, February 5, was cold and rainy. There had come, in that first week of February, a warm spell that had melted the snow north of Kaskaskia and made the rivers rise. With each day of rain, they were higher. Some were already over their banks and spreading out on the prairie.

They set out in the afternoon of the 5th in the grayness of drizzle. The next day it rained so hard that they stayed in camp.

"Maybe the sun will shine tomorrow," said Major Joseph Bowman, the officer on whom Clark counted the most for help. But it didn't, and camp was broken in wetness, above, below and all around the men.

Major Bowman kept notes in which he said it was still raining on February 10.

Every little stream had become a wide river. The men crossed each of them holding their rifles and powder horns over their heads. If either got wet, it was useless. So they trudged along, one hundred thirty men, followed by a few packhorses to carry extra supplies. Much of the time they walked in water or mud halfway to their knees. The men shot game along the way, and there was usually meat to be cooked on sticks when they made camp. Clark did not mind the men hunting along the way.

"Gives them something to think about besides how miserable they feel sloshing through this endless mud," Clark said to Bowman. "And fresh meat is good food for a man to march on."

On February 13th, they reached the edge of what appeared to be a lake at least five miles wide.

"This must be the Little Wabash, but it certainly doesn't live up to its name," Clark said. There was usually a stretch of land about three miles wide between the Little Wabash and the Wabash. Now both rivers were over their banks and had become one great sheet of water. This was the chosen place for the meeting with the gunboat. They made camp on the last rise of ground before the "lake."

Clark watched for a messenger from the gunboat. None came, either the first day or the next two. He learned later that Indians had attacked the gunboat, and John Rogers had been among those killed. At the end of three days, Clark knew that he would have to go on without the men and supplies the boat had carried. The attack on Fort Sackville would have to be made without the cannons. Furthermore, they would have to cross all this water without the boat.

The first day in camp, he had the men take a dugout canoe, in which scouts went out. They were to watch for a patrol scouting from the fort, and to find a place for the next camp.

"Nothing stirring up that way at all," the scouts reported. "We found a place, about half an acre, that's not too bad for camping."

"Fine," said Clark. "Now let's get some good stout poles cut and build a platform on the other side of the Little Wabash channel. We'll take the loads from the pack train there by boat and swim the horses over to where the loads will be above water again."

Soon the men were in the ferryboat business. They had built a second canoe while they waited in camp. They entered into the boating back and forth in good spirits. A fourteen-year-old drummer boy set them all to laughing when he found himself in water too deep and sat on his drum, poling himself through the water.

Colonel Clark needed a good laugh about that time. Young Willie, the drummer boy, seeing his leader's concern, said, "Don't worry, Colonel Clark. We came this far and we can make it all the way up to the gates of the fort — and inside them, too!"

"Either inside the fort gates or inside the pearly gates," remarked one of the soldiers. But he grinned as he said it.

This good feeling, and a spirit of helping each other, took them through the next days. They waded for miles in water up to the armpits. The canoes were used only where it was impossible for men to walk holding their rifles and powder horns high, and to help those who were weak from the long days of being wet and cold.

They moved slowly from a camp at one rise of land to another, always wet, always cold, always hungry. They had to leave the pack train behind, at last, and the food was all gone. Most of the game animals had fled before the floodwaters. One night the men found a fox on their camping hill. Its flesh was bitter, but they ate it just the same. They had two good feasts, when they camped at places where the opossums had flocked to escape the waters.

"Here's our dinner!" the first men to see the little frightened animals called out. "Come on, fellows! 'Possum stew tonight!"

By February 20, they could hear the guns boom at the opening of the day at Fort Sackville. Wading, swimming, pulling themselves from bush to bush, somehow the men struggled through the last flooded miles. They had crossed the Wabash now, and on February 24 they were near enough to Vincennes to hear faintly the sounds from the town. In the afternoon, the sun began to shine.

"A good sign!" one of the men said, and they all agreed.

Some Frenchmen from Vincennes were out hunting ducks just ahead of the Americans, who watched from a woodland. One hunter got off his horse as he came near. Clark called to him. He came, not seeming to be alarmed at the sight of the dirty, bearded men.

"Americans!" he said.

"Yes," said Clark. "We are ready to bring liberty to the people of Vincennes. Will you help us?"

The hunter seemed willing. He answered all the

questions the tall, mud-spattered man with the red beard asked him. When he left to go back to town, he carried with him a card on which Clark had written a note to be shown at each house in the town. It asked each family to stay inside while the attack was taking place, and threatened severe punishment for any person who raised arms against the Americans outside the fort. The hunter's eyes sparkled as he rode away with the card hidden inside his jacket. He was going to enjoy the important part he was about to play.

From the woods, Clark watched the town anxiously. Some of the people came running out to try to see the Americans, but it seemed that no one in the fort noticed this. He learned later that a lady whose husband was a prisoner in the fort took some supper to him and whispered the news. Her husband whispered it to Captain Helm who was also a prisoner.

Captain Helm and General Hamilton had become quite good friends, and often whiled away the long evenings by playing cards before the fire in the general's house. This evening, Captain Helm made sure that he kept the general's attention on the card game and that the general had plenty of Helm's favorite drink, apple toddy.

As the day ended, Clark sent the Cahokia militia

ahead to see that all was well in the town. They looked just like the townspeople, except for an extra share of mud, and they spoke French so they did not attract much attention. As darkness came, all the rest of the men approached the town. As they took positions from which to fire into the fort, the Cahokia men gave most of them a bit of roast duck and bread, sent by the Vincennes housewives.

In trees, in the log church steeple, behind walls and large tree trunks, only a few yards from the log palisades of Fort Sackville, Clark's men hid in readiness for a signal from their leader. There were cracks between the logs, and holes left for the men in the fort to fire through. A rifle was aimed at each of these, and the sharpshooting frontiersmen's aim was true.

Inside General Hamilton's house, Helm fumbled the cards a little as he dealt them, but General Hamilton did not notice. Then there was a sudden sound of rifle fire. Hamilton jumped up.

"Sit down, General," Helm said. "Don't let some drunken Indian spoil our game."

Hamilton sat down, but he kept looking toward the door nervously as the game began. "Those shots were close," he said.

Helm said, "Now just because you happen to have

a bad hand, don't use a little horseplay out there as an excuse to get out of playing the hand."

The game went on for another minute, when there was a second round of firing.

"I'm going out to investigate," Hamilton said, getting up.

Helm shrugged his shoulders and followed. He had tried.

On the parade ground, a sergeant had fallen, struck by fire. He was only stunned, however, for the round Kentucky bullet had hit him squarely on a brass button on his red coat. He could only point toward the palisade walls to show where the bullet had come from.

Hamilton barked orders and the British soldiers began the defense of Fort Sackville. Just as they decided that the enemy was on one side of the fort, the firing would come from another direction. Again the direction would change. Clark had his men all around the fort, and used the change of direction to try to convince Hamilton that there were many companies attacking. He also had told the men to bring flags with them from Kaskaskia, and these were now mounted on long poles, cut in the woods as the men waited there, and placed around the town.

About four in the morning, the firing slowed, but at dawn it began again. Hearing a great deal of shouting, and firing from so many directions, Hamilton was sure that a large army surrounded him. How they could have come through all that high water, the general could not understand. However they had arrived and their aim was deadly. They seemed able to find every crack in the fort walls. Many of his men had been hit. Their shots could only be aimed in the general direction from which the firing came, as the men couldn't see the hiding frontiersmen.

About nine o'clock, Clark sent a messenger, carrying a white flag, with the first surrender demand. Hamilton refused it. Immediately, the inside of the fort was peppered from all sides and above. The British soldiers could find no safe positions from which to fire.

At noon, the firing from inside the fort stopped, and a white flag appeared above the gate. Clark signaled a cease-fire for his men. He had been truly worried lest his men be forced to stop firing for lack of ammunition before this happened, and that moment was close. It would have come much sooner, had it not been that friends in Vincennes had hidden gunpowder and given it to Clark the night before.

"Look who it is!" Simon Kenton nudged Colonel Clark. "Our old friend, Leonard Helm!"

Captain Helm, his eyes twinkling, marched up to Clark. "Sir, General Hamilton requests that you come inside the fort to discuss terms."

"You tell him to meet me out here, on the parade ground. If he's not willing to do that, I'll order my reserves up and we'll really see the bullets fly." Clark looked right at Helm as he said this, though he knew that Leonard was aware that he was bluffing. Helm, his back to the fort, winked before he turned about and marched back inside.

Soon General Hamilton met Clark outside the fort and the terms of surrender were arranged. It became official the next morning, February 25, 1779. The Illinois Country was won for the United States. Vincennes became a capital of Indiana Territory a few years later, and when Illinois became a state in 1818, Kaskaskia was the first capital city.

It didn't just happen that way. It came about because men like LaSalle, Tonty and Clark could dream and plan and because there were men of courage to make the dreams come true.